End Every Addiction:

Quickly and Easily Without Withdrawal or Relapse

Dr. Jeffrey J. Rodman, LPC, LSATP, CCMHt

End Every Addiction: Quickly and Easily without Withdrawal or Relapse

Copyright © 2023 by Dr. Jeffrey J. Rodman, LPC, LSATP, CCMHt
All Rights Reserved
No part of this book may be reproduced or transmitted in any form or by any means whatsoever without express written permission from the author, except in the case of brief quotations embodied in critical articles and reviews. Please refer all pertinent questions to the publisher.

End Every Addiction: Quickly and Easily without Withdrawal or Relapse

Table of Contents

Dedication 5

Foreword 6

Client Vignettes: An Important Note 9

Introduction 11

   SECTION ONE: UNDERSTANDING ADDICTION 16

Chapter 1: Types of Addiction: Substance, Process, People, Thought, and Emotional Addictions 17

Chapter 2: Cautions While Detoxing and the Risk of Starting Suboxone 31

Chapter 3: Three (Maybe Four) Prerequisites to Ending Every Addiction 41

   SECTION TWO: UNDERSTANDING THE MIND 51

Chapter 4: The Radical Cause Concept: Taking Responsibility for Your Life 52

Chapter 5: Understanding Abraham Maslow's Hierarchy of Needs 61

Chapter 6: Understanding the Neurological Levels of the Mind 68

Chapter 7: End Addiction by Shifting Thinking Using Psycho-Cybernetics 93

SECTION THREE: UNDERSTANDING ADDICTION INTERVENTIONS 100

Chapter 8: Taking Responsibility for Your Own Addiction Recovery 101

Chapter 9: Ending Addiction Through Mindfulness Practice 107

Chapter 10: Techniques for Managing Negative Thoughts and Emotions 115

Chapter 11: Effective Therapeutic Approaches to End Any Addiction 129

SECTION FOUR: UNDERSTANDING RELAPSE PREVENTION 144

Chapter 12: Setting an Intention for the Life You Want to Live After You Recover 145

Chapter 13: Permanent Relapse Prevention Strategies After Ending an Addiction 155

Chapter 14: The Pros and Cons of 12-Step Programs . 180

Chapter 15: Wrapping it Up 192

Dedication

To My Dearest Wife and Children,

I am forever grateful for your unwavering love and support throughout the years. You have been the constant source of inspiration and joy in my life, and I can't thank you enough for being my rock.

Writing this book would not have been possible without your understanding and encouragement. Your unwavering belief in me has given me the confidence to pursue my dreams and write this book.

To my wife, thank you for being my partner in life, my best friend, and my soulmate. Your love and care have been the foundation of our family, and I admire your strength and commitment to our marriage and children.

To my children, you are the light of my life. Watching you grow up and become the amazing individuals you are today has been the greatest joy of my life. I hope this book inspires you to chase your dreams and never give up on what you believe.

My family has been my motivation to push through life's challenges. I love you all to the moon and back.

With all my love!

Foreword

By: Michael Stevenson

As a Master Practitioner in the field of human transformation, I have come across numerous books offering solutions for those who suffer from addiction. However, none resonated with me quite like "End Every Addiction" by Dr. Jeffrey J. Rodman.

In this book, Dr. Rodman takes a unique approach to addiction recovery by going beyond the traditional idea of simply leading people from addiction to recovery. Instead, he guides readers to complete freedom from addiction, offering practical solutions to help readers achieve a healthy and balanced life.

What sets Dr. Rodman's approach apart is the use of advanced human change approaches such as hypnotherapy, Neuro-Linguistic Programming (NLP), Eye Movement Integration (EMI), and addressing the root causes of addiction. These innovative techniques help readers achieve a complete transformation and break the cycle of addiction.

Drawing on his extensive experience working with patients suffering from various addictions, Dr. Rodman's holistic approach to recovery provides a deep understanding of the psychological and biological components of addiction and recovery.

One of the things that impressed me most about this book is Dr. Rodman's ability to explain complex theories and concepts in a straightforward, relatable manner. His writing style is engaging and easy to understand, making this book a valuable resource for anyone in the field of addiction recovery.

Throughout the book, Dr. Rodman stresses the importance of personal responsibility and improving mental and physical health as crucial parts of successfully moving from addiction recovery toward freedom from addiction. He provides practical strategies for reducing stress, improving mindfulness, improving sleep, and creating positive lifestyle habits - all crucial steps to help End Every Addiction.

Whether you are a person struggling with addiction, a family member or loved one looking to understand addiction better, or a professional seeking to improve your knowledge of addiction recovery, "End Every Addiction" is a must-read. I highly recommend this book to anyone looking for insightful and practical guidance on achieving and maintaining freedom from addiction.

Sincerely,

Michael Stevenson, MNLP, MTT, MHt

Founder and President, Transform Destiny and Ethical Marketing Academy

#1 Best-Selling Author: "Becoming Positively Awesome" and "Learn Hypnosis... Now!"

Client Vignettes: An Important Note

As you delve into the stories and experiences outlined in the following pages, it's critical to understand some key aspects about the client vignettes included. These vignettes provide an invaluable insight into the various scenarios and challenges encountered, and they serve as practical examples to illuminate the principles and strategies discussed.

First and foremost, it is important to note that the privacy and confidentiality of my clients is a paramount concern. Consequently, all names used in these stories have been changed to protect the identities of the individuals involved. Any resemblance to actual persons, living or dead, or actual events is purely coincidental.

Moreover, some of the vignettes may not represent a single individual but rather a composite of various clients. This approach ensures a broader representation of situations and issues. By amalgamating multiple experiences, I present a more comprehensive picture of the diverse circumstances people face. This allows a wider range of topics and solutions to be covered, offering a richer understanding of the subject matter.

So, as you read these vignettes, remember that while they are rooted in real-life experiences, they have been modified and molded to serve the greater purpose of this book: to educate, empower, and inspire.

Introduction

When people think of addiction they usually think of a hopeless alcoholic living on the streets or a nodding out heroin addict.

The Merriam-Webster Dictionary defines addiction as "a compulsive, chronic, physiological or psychological need for a habit-forming substance, behavior, or activity having harmful physical, psychological, or social effects and typically causing well-defined symptoms (such as anxiety, irritability, tremors, or nausea) upon withdrawal or abstinence[1]."

The truth is, we can, and do, become addicted to a wide variety of substances, things, behaviors, individuals, and even thought patterns. At its core, addiction is less about the substance or behavior itself and more about the underlying psychological and emotional factors that drive us to engage in these behaviors. In other words, what we become addicted to is ourselves—or rather, the self that we have been programmed to be.

---

[1] Merriam-Webster Dictionary, s.v. "Addiction," accessed August 26, 2021, https://www.merriam-webster.com/dictionary/addiction.

This programming begins early on in life as we learn coping mechanisms for dealing with stress and emotions. The programming that leads to addictive behavior can begin early on in life, even before we are born. Generational traumas, such as poverty, abuse, or addiction itself, can be passed down from generation to generation and impact our earliest experiences of the world. These traumas may shape our coping mechanisms for dealing with stress and emotions and make us more vulnerable to addictive behaviors later in life. It is important to recognize the role that early experiences play in shaping our relationship with substances and behaviors to break free from these patterns.

For some of us, this programming can lead us down a path of addictive behavior as we seek relief from uncomfortable feelings like anxiety or depression. When we engage in behaviors that bring us pleasure or relieve stress, our brains release natural chemicals like dopamine that make us feel good. Over time, repeated engagement in these behaviors can change the structure of our brains so that we become more sensitive to these pleasurable chemicals.

This sensitivity can lead to a vicious cycle of addiction. As we try to achieve the previous level of pleasure, we seek out increasingly extreme experiences. Doing this releases the same chemicals from the same pleasure centers as before. Because our brains are wired to seek out pleasure and to avoid pain, it can be difficult to break free from this cycle once it has taken hold.

But perhaps even more importantly, breaking free from addiction requires a fundamental shift in how we view ourselves and our relationship with the world around us. We need to rewire our brains and create new neural pathways that lead us toward new outcomes and a new self. Since the addiction is an addiction to the self, we need to shed the old self and create a new identity and a new self that gets us more of the results we want in life. By learning healthy coping mechanisms for dealing with stress and emotions, cultivating supportive relationships with others who share our values and goals, and finding meaning and purpose in life beyond addictive behaviors, we can begin to reprogram ourselves toward a healthier way of being.

In short, addiction isn't just about drugs, alcohol, sex, gambling, shopping, video games, pornography, grief, or anything else. It is about who we are at the core of our identity. By taking steps toward greater self-awareness and personal growth, we can break free from the chains of addiction and live a life full of meaning and purpose.

We can shed the old self that no longer serves us and create a new self and a new identity that gets us the life we want.

In the process of breaking your addiction to the self, it will be critical to end every addiction. This means removing every addiction from your mind, from your body, and from your very identity. It isn't enough to switch to less harmful addictions, less offensive addictions, or to more socially acceptable addictions. You need to actually eliminate addiction from your system so that it no longer stands as a barrier between your current self and the new self you are becoming. You will actually discard the old self that is stuck in harmful and destructive thinking, feeling, and behavior patterns to create a new identity that supports a healthy self-concept aligned with health, success, prosperity, and freedom.

Substance addictions, process addictions, people addictions, thought addictions, and emotional addictions all control your life in such a way as to prevent one from becoming self-actualized, becoming ones true self, and meeting the full potential of which they have been endowed.

To understand how to end every addiction I have organized this book into four sections:

- Section One is about understanding addiction
- Section Two is about understanding the mind
- Section Three outlines the specific interventions used to end every addiction
- Section Four addresses relapse prevention

SECTION ONE: UNDERSTANDING ADDICTION

Chapter 1: Types of Addiction: Substance, Process, People, Thought, and Emotional Addictions

Addiction is a complex phenomenon that can take many different forms. Understanding the similarities and differences between various types of addiction can be helpful in understanding how best to overcome this condition. At a basic level, all addictions share commonalities such as compulsive behaviors, obsessive thinking, and difficulty controlling the urge to use despite negative consequences. In addition, there is a great deal of overlap between the different types of addictions. Substance addiction always has process and emotional addiction components. Every type of addiction triggers the release of chemicals in the body. An individual's dependence is often more closely tied to the chemicals triggered than to the chemicals ingested or behaviors acted upon.

Substance Addictions

Substance addictions occur when drugs or alcohol are used with excessive frequency and in a manner that disrupts normal functioning. Substance addictions occur when an individual begins to depend on drugs or alcohol to the point that it severely disrupts their daily life. This type of addiction typically involves recurrent and compulsive use of substances such as opioid painkillers, marijuana, stimulants, or alcohol despite experiencing negative consequences. The frequency of use often leads to physical dependence, tolerance, and if the substance is suddenly discontinued, withdrawal.

There are several types of drugs and substances that can lead to addiction. Some of these include:

> Alcohol
> Alcohol is the most commonly abused substance worldwide.[2] It is legal for adults over the age of 21 in many countries but can be highly addictive if consumed in excess. Alcohol addiction can cause

---

[2] World Health Organization, "Alcohol," accessed August 26, 2021, https://www.who.int/health-topics/alcohol#tab=tab_1

physical symptoms, such as liver damage, high blood pressure, and heart disease. According to the Substance Abuse and Mental Health Services Administration (SAMHSA), alcohol is the drug that people most often seek treatment for, accounting for nearly 40% of all admissions to substance abuse treatment facilities.[3]

Marijuana

Marijuana is a psychoactive drug derived from the cannabis plant that is illegal under federal law. In addition to being the illicit drug most commonly abused by the general population[4], marijuana is also the most common illicit drug used by those seeking treatment, accounting for almost 20% of admissions.[5]

---

[3] Substance Abuse and Mental Health Services Administration. (2019). Treatment Episode Data Set (TEDS): 2017. Admissions to and Discharges from Publicly-Funded Substance Use Treatment. Rockville, MD: Substance Abuse and Mental Health Services Administration.

[4] Substance Abuse and Mental Health Services Administration. (2019). Key Substance Use and Mental Health Indicators in the United States: Results from the 2018 National Survey on Drug Use and Health. Rockville, MD: Center for Behavioral Health Statistics and Quality, Substance Abuse and Mental Health Services Administration.

[5] Substance Abuse and Mental Health Services Administration. (2019). Treatment Episode Data Set (TEDS): 2017. Admissions to and Discharges from Publicly-Funded Substance Use Treatment. Rockville, MD: Substance Abuse and Mental Health Services Administration.

Marijuana use can lead to dependence if used frequently over time. Marijuana use has been associated with Amotivational Syndrome, state-dependent learning, and memory loss. Amotivational Syndrome is a condition that affects motivation and drive, leading to decreased productivity and interest in activities. State-dependent learning occurs when information learned while under the influence of marijuana can only be recalled when the individual is also under the influence. Memory loss is another potential side effect of marijuana use, especially in heavy or long-term users.

Opioids
Opioids include prescription painkillers, such as oxycodone, hydrocodone, codeine, morphine, and fentanyl. They are often prescribed for chronic pain management but can be highly addictive if not taken as directed by a medical professional. Illegal opioids are synthetic or semi-synthetic drugs that are not prescribed by a doctor and are typically used for non-medical purposes. Examples include heroin, fentanyl, and carfentanil. These drugs are highly addictive and can cause a range of serious health problems, including respiratory depression, heart failure, and overdose. Opioid addiction can cause severe

withdrawal symptoms such as nausea, vomiting, diarrhea, anxiety, and depression.

Stimulants
Stimulants include drugs, such as cocaine, amphetamines, and methamphetamine. They are commonly abused for their euphoric effects and ability to increase energy levels and alertness. Stimulant addiction can cause physical symptoms such as rapid heartbeat, high blood pressure, and insomnia.

Depressants
Depressants include drugs, such as benzodiazepines (Xanax, Valium) and barbiturates (phenobarbital). They are often prescribed for anxiety disorders but can be highly addictive if misused or taken without a prescription. Depressant addiction can cause severe withdrawal symptoms, such as seizures and hallucinations.

Other Over-the-counter supplements
While not all supplements are considered addictive, some may contain ingredients that could be harmful when consumed excessively. For example, caffeine pills or energy drinks may contain high amounts of caffeine which could lead to jitters, nervousness,

headaches, elevated blood pressure, etc. Other supplements should only be taken under advice from a doctor because they could interfere with other medications you might be taking. Melatonin is one such supplement.

Kratom is another supplement that has gained popularity recently, and it has been associated with negative side effects including addiction and withdrawal symptoms.

Process Addictions

Process addictions involve compulsively engaging in certain activities leading to a strong experience of gratification, even when there are negative consequences.

Some examples of these activities include:

- Watching pornography
- Gambling
- Shopping
- Excessive video game playing
- Binging, purging, and other eating disorder-related behaviors
- Workaholism

- Obsessive and unhealthy sexual activity
- Excessive use of mobile phones
- Other behavioral patterns

Over time, the individual may become more dependent on these activities as they become more entrenched in the addictive cycle. Process addictions do not result in physical dependency per se but do often result in a dependence on the release of chemicals produced by our body. Process addictions can also cause severe psychological impacts such as increased anxiety or depression often associated with impulsivity or difficulty controlling impulses. Treatment plans for process addictions should involve understanding potential triggers and developing healthy coping strategies.

It is essential to recognize the signs and symptoms of process addictions so the person can seek treatment before the addiction becomes deeply entrenched. Some common indications of process addiction include:

- Spending excessive time on the activity
- Neglecting responsibilities or social relationships
- Difficulty controlling impulses related to the behavior
- Engaging in the activity despite negative consequences
- Feeling shame or guilt about the behavior

Individuals with process addictions often experience a powerful sense of gratification from their behavior. This feeling is due to the release of chemicals produced by our body that creates a sensation of being high. Over time, these individuals may become more dependent on these activities as they become more entrenched in the addictive cycle.

Emotional Addictions

Emotional addictions are becoming increasingly common in today's society, with some people becoming overly dependent on negative emotions or external factors for emotional support and validation. This type of addiction typically arises from an individual's inability to manage their own emotions effectively and the need to seek comfort in external sources.

Emotional addiction is a phenomenon where people become addicted to certain emotions or feelings as a means of coping with their lives. It can manifest in many forms, such as relying on depression or anxiety to soothe oneself or seeking emotional security by depending on another person. In these cases, the individual may continue to hold onto negative emotions as a means of protecting themselves from the discomfort of change or uncertainty. Emotional addiction can have harmful consequences, as it can lead to a perpetuation of negative patterns of thinking and behavior and prevent individuals from leading fulfilling lives. It is important to recognize the signs of emotional addiction and seek help if necessary to break free from these patterns and develop healthier coping mechanisms.

Two of the most powerful negative emotions that contribute to emotional addiction are guilt/shame and grief. Individuals who struggle with guilt/shame may rely on these feelings as a way to punish themselves or feel like they deserve punishment. Similarly, individuals who experience grief may become addicted to the feeling of sadness, finding comfort in the familiarity of their pain.

It is important to recognize the signs of an emotional addiction and take the steps needed to build healthy coping mechanisms to ensure long-term successful recovery.

Some common symptoms of emotional addiction include:

- Feeling unable to control one's emotions
- Relying heavily on outside sources for emotional

support
- Finding it difficult to function without experiencing intense negative emotions
- Engaging in self-destructive behaviors as a way to cope with negative emotions

Breaking free from an emotional addiction is not easy, but it is possible with dedication and effort. By recognizing the signs of an emotional addiction and taking proactive steps toward recovery, individuals can learn how to manage their own emotions effectively and build healthy coping mechanisms for long-term success.

Thought Addictions

Thought Addictions occur when people get addicted to negative thinking patterns and negative thought loops. When people become addicted to negative thinking, they often ruminate on past mistakes or worry about future events that may never happen. This type of thinking can be difficult to break free from, but it is important to recognize when it is happening and take steps to change the pattern. By focusing on positive thoughts and practicing mindfulness techniques, individuals can break free from their thought addictions and cultivate a more positive outlook on life.

Thought addictions can have a significant impact on an individual's mental health and well-being. They can lead to feelings of anxiety, depression, poor self-image, and low self-esteem. The good news is that with awareness and practice, it is possible to break free from these addictive patterns and cultivate a more positive outlook on life. The first step in breaking free from thought addictions is recognizing when they are occurring.

Some common signs of thought addiction include:

- Inability to let go of past mistakes or regrets
- Constant worry about the future
- Negative self-talk or self-criticism
- Obsessive thoughts or rumination

People Addictions

People addictions can take many forms, but they all share one common trait: a dangerous cycle of self-destructive behavior. Love/sex addiction, codependency, relationships, self-help groups, and even violent interactions with another person can all lead down this path.

Relationship addiction is perhaps the most well-known form of people addiction. Those who suffer from relationship addiction may jump from one relationship to another in search of fulfillment or validation. This constant need for companionship can be exhausting and ultimately lead to a lack of meaningful connections with others.

Love/sex addiction is characterized by an obsessive need for attention and validation from others. This can manifest in a variety of ways, such as compulsively seeking out sexual encounters or constantly pursuing romantic relationships. While it may seem harmless on the surface, love/sex addiction can lead to a host of negative consequences, including damaged relationships and emotional instability.

Codependency is another form of people addiction that involves an unhealthy reliance on others for one's sense of self-worth. Codependent individuals often sacrifice their own needs and desires in order to please others, leading to feelings of resentment and frustration over time.

Self-help groups are often seen as a positive way to overcome personal struggles, but they too can become addictive in nature. Some individuals may become overly reliant on these groups for support and guidance, leading to an unhealthy dependency on them.

Finally, violent interactions with another person,

whether physical or emotional, can also be considered a form of people addiction. Those who engage in such behavior often experience a rush of adrenaline or power which leads them down a dangerous path toward further aggression.

People addictions are very real and should not be taken lightly. They have the potential to cause just as much harm as substance abuse if left unchecked. People addictions can cause immense pain and suffering to those involved and it's important to recognize the signs of addiction before it gets out of control.

People who are addicted to relationships, for example, may find it difficult to maintain healthy boundaries in their interactions with others. They may become fixated on a certain person, overly dependent on them, and experience extreme feelings of loneliness when the relationship is over. Codependency can also be a problem in addiction—allowing someone else to control and manipulate your life to fill an inner void. Other forms of people addiction such as love/sex addiction and violence can lead to serious physical and psychological harm, not only to the sufferer but also those around them. Self-help groups and therapy are possible courses of action for those seeking relief from their addictions.

There are also differences between these types of

addiction. Substance abuse tends to result in physical dependence as well as tolerance, which requires more frequent use to achieve the desired effect. Process addictions may not result in physical withdrawal symptoms but can have severe emotional consequences if gone unchecked. For instance, gambling may lead to significant financial losses while excessive shopping can cause debt accumulation or family conflicts due to unwise spending habits. Emotional addictions put a heavy psychological burden on those involved due to feelings of insecurity and lack of trust caused by constant comparisons between oneself and others.

All addictions are serious conditions that require a well-developed approach to recovery and often help from trained professionals who can provide support tailored to each individual's needs. Understanding the similarities and differences between the different kinds of addictions can help individuals recognize their own patterns of behavior so they can make changes and move forward with their lives free from the grip of addiction.

Chapter 2: Cautions While Detoxing and the Risk of Starting Suboxone

Detoxing from drugs can be a crucial step in recovery, but it is also one that comes with a certain amount of caution. In particular, those who are detoxing from substances like alcohol and opiates should be aware of the potential risks of serious or fatal complications.

Other types of drugs that can cause serious issues during detox include benzodiazepines like Xanax and Valium, and stimulants like cocaine and methamphetamine.

While not all of these drugs carry an immediate risk of death while detoxing, they can still cause severe withdrawal symptoms which may lead to more serious health issues if not managed properly. This is why it is extremely important to always seek professional medical advice before attempting any kind of detox.

I always work closely with a client's primary care doctor to ensure they are properly weaned off substances as quickly as possible while still maintaining health and safety.

****

My client, Colin, struggled with opioid addiction. After several failed attempts at quitting, Colin decided to seek help from a medical professional. The doctor prescribed him Suboxone, which is a medication used to treat opioid addiction and alleviate withdrawal symptoms.

At first, Colin was grateful for the help of Suboxone. It made the withdrawal process much easier and allowed him to focus on getting his life back on track. However, as the weeks turned into months and then into years, Colin found himself still dependent on Suboxone and felt like he could no longer advance on his journey of self-improvement.

He had gone from one addiction to another, but this time the drug was legal and prescribed. Colin felt his life slipping through his fingers once again. He had become "stuck" with Suboxone and didn't know how to get off the medication.

Colin confided in his doctor about his concerns. His

doctor told him that his dependence on Suboxone was a common side effect of long-term use and that he should stay the course. The doctor recommended gradually tapering off the medication, but Colin found that every time he reduced his dose, the withdrawal symptoms became unbearable.

He felt hopeless and trapped, and that he would never escape the clutches of Suboxone. However, one day, he stumbled across my services for individuals who were struggling with similar issues. Through hypnotherapy, mindfulness training, and brain retraining, and with continued effort, Colin was able to wean himself off Suboxone in only 3 weeks. Quickly and easily, he realized that he had the strength to overcome his addiction, and he was grateful for the newfound freedom he had gained in his life.

****

It is important to understand that when it comes to detoxing from any substance, there is no one-size-fits-all approach. Each person will have unique needs and requirements depending on his/her situation. That said, there are some key things to keep in mind when it comes to making sure the detoxification process is as safe as possible.

First, do not attempt a DIY detox. Always seek

professional medical advice before attempting any form of drug detox, as some drugs carry risks associated with them such as seizures and breathing difficulties if done incorrectly. Make sure you have access to medical help. Do not try to do it alone; make sure you always have support nearby during your detox process.

When talking to your doctor about detoxing from any of the substances mentioned above, you may want to discuss the potential risks involved with detoxing without medication. Your doctor can provide information and guidance based on your individual circumstances and health needs, as well as advice on how best to manage mild withdrawal symptoms. Depending on the severity of your situation, medications may be prescribed to help mitigate any potential dangers associated with detoxing and to help manage your symptoms more effectively.

It is important to emphasize to your doctor that you want to achieve both the safe and effective management of withdrawal symptoms while minimizing the number of medications you take and getting off them as quickly as possible. Be sure your doctor understands that you are not interested in long-term medication assisted treatment but only in minimizing the safety risks of detoxing too quickly.

Understand the withdrawal symptoms associated with your particular drug(s) of choice and learn how best to manage them. These can range from insomnia and anxiety to muscle aches and nausea. If they become too difficult or unmanageable, seeking medical advice should be your priority.

The timeline for achieving a full recovery and becoming 100% drug and medication free will vary depending on individual circumstances. Most clients I have worked with can be weaned off Suboxone in 2-4 weeks. Factors such as how long you have been using the substances, the severity of your addiction, and any underlying mental health conditions can all affect how quickly you are able to recover. Your doctor should be able to provide more information based on your individual situation and answer any questions you have about your recovery timeline. Establish a plan for what you will do after your detox has been completed. Having a relapse prevention strategy in place will help ensure a sturdy foundation for long-term sobriety.

Detoxing from any kind of substance requires caution and care for it to be successful without putting yourself at risk for physical harm or relapse back into addiction. Following the guidelines above can help provide you with safety measures that can protect your physical well-being while allowing you the space needed for healing and renewal.

Medication Assisted Treatment (MAT)

If you have researched addiction treatment, you have most likely found Medication Assisted Treatment to be the most widely promoted approach.

Medication Assisted Treatment (MAT) is commonly recommended for managing substance withdrawal symptoms and forms a core part of many addiction treatment programs. MAT involves the use of FDA-approved medications to help reduce or eliminate cravings and control the side effects that can be experienced during detoxification from drugs or alcohol.

MAT originated as Methadone Management, which was the first medication approved for the treatment of opioid addiction in the United States. Suboxone was introduced later and was initially seen as a significant advancement in the field of addiction treatment. However, it has since become a double-edged sword, as some patients may become dependent on it for years. This has led to concerns about whether MAT practitioners are enabling dependency instead of helping people overcome addiction. While MAT can be an effective tool in treating addiction, it's important to ensure that it is used appropriately as a short-term detoxification tool.

Originally, Medication Assisted Treatment with Suboxone was intended to be used for only 2-4 weeks as part of an overall detoxification process. During this time frame, it helps reduce cravings and withdrawal symptoms while providing the user with a sense of stability during their transition from other addictive substances.

It's important to remember that while Suboxone can be effective in helping people manage their addiction and get clean, it is not meant to be used as a long-term solution. If it is used beyond the recommended short-term period, there is an increased risk of potential side effects such as dependence or tolerance - which could ultimately lead to triggering the relapse cycle again and again.

Do Not Do It Alone

It's important to realize that getting off Suboxone successfully will require help from others. Find a practitioner who understands addiction, will meet your individual needs, and provide support throughout the process. This can be especially helpful if you have any coexisting conditions such as trauma, anxiety, or depression, which may affect how you respond to the process.

Gradual Reduction Schedule

Rather than trying to quit cold turkey, it is best to gradually reduce your dosage over time to avoid triggering acute withdrawal symptoms. Your doctor and therapist should work with you to create a tailored schedule for reducing your dose over two to four weeks - depending on your individual needs.

Nutritional Supplements that Help with Withdrawal

When going through withdrawal, it's important to take care of your body and ensure that you're eating a healthy diet and getting enough rest. Additionally, there are certain nutritional supplements that may be beneficial in mitigating withdrawal symptoms. Some of these include:

- Omega-3 fatty acids
  Omega-3s can help reduce inflammation in the brain, which can make withdrawal more

manageable.
- Magnesium
Magnesium helps to relax muscles and ease tension, which can help reduce cravings.
- Vitamin B6 & B12
These vitamins help with mood regulation and energy levels, both of which are important for managing withdrawal symptoms.
- L-glutamine
This amino acid is known for its ability to reduce anxiety and boost mood.
- Probiotics
Probiotics may provide a boost of good bacteria in the gut, which can aid in nutrient absorption during detoxification.
- Potassium
Potassium is an electrolyte mineral that plays an important role in the body, especially during times of stress like withdrawal. Low potassium levels can lead to fatigue, muscle cramps, and dizziness; all of which are common symptoms of Suboxone withdrawal.

It is recommended that individuals increase their potassium during detoxification to maintain a healthy balance and to support the process. Good sources of potassium include leafy green vegetables, bananas, avocados, and potatoes. Additionally, daily multivitamins may also provide beneficial amounts of potassium.

Chapter 3: Three (Maybe Four) Prerequisites to Ending Every Addiction

No one should ever have to go through the pain and suffering that addiction brings. Fortunately, it is possible to end an addiction with the right plan and dedication. But before you can make any real progress in ending your addiction, there are three—maybe four—critical prerequisites.

Believe It Is Possible

One of the most important steps toward ending an addiction is believing that it's actually possible to do so. If you don't believe that it can be done, your motivation will be likely to wane and it will be difficult for you to really focus on achieving recovery. For you to have a fighting chance at sobriety, you must believe that with a positive mindset and determination, you can overcome your addiction.

****

I recently had a client, Jack, who had grown up in a family of addicts. His father and grandfather both battled addiction for most of their lives, and he had seen countless others in his community struggle as well. As a result, Jack had never truly believed that it was possible to overcome addiction.

Jack had begun his struggle with addiction in his early twenties. He had tried everything from rehab to therapy to medication, but nothing seemed to work. He felt hopeless and defeated, convinced that he would be battling his addiction for the rest of his life.

Then Jack stumbled upon an article online about someone who had successfully overcome addiction. He couldn't believe it at first because the subject of the article had a remarkably similar story to his own. How could someone actually beat this thing? But as he read more stories of recovery and watched videos of people sharing their experiences, something inside him started to shift.

For the first time in years, Jack began to believe that recovery was possible. It wasn't going to be easy - he knew that much - but if others could do it, then maybe he could too.

****

Believe You Can Do It

Not only do you need to believe that it's possible to end every addiction, but you also need to believe that it is possible for you specifically. This requires faith in yourself and in your ability to recover and stay recovered once you have removed addiction from your mind and body. Often, we believe other people can end their addiction, but we may have less belief in ourselves.

Maybe you just can't imagine yourself free of your addiction. Maybe you feel like you are too far gone; a lost cause, entangled, and hopelessly addicted until the day you die. You may even think addiction is your destiny. It can be very difficult if feelings of self-doubt creep in, which is why it is important to have a comprehensive mind-body based approach as well as strong support from people who care about you.

****

After reading an article online and feeling a newfound sense of hope, Jack began to research different

treatment options. He found my practice and was immediately drawn to my approach of combining traditional therapy with holistic practices like meditation and mindfulness. He reached out to me for an initial consultation, and we talked about his history with addiction and his goals for recovery.

With this newfound hope and determination, Jack committed himself fully to the new treatment options I offered him and to the recovery process. There were setbacks along the way, but every time he felt like giving up, he reminded himself that others had overcome similar struggles before him.

****

Decide

Once you believe change is possible and that change is possible for you, it is now time to decide that you want this for yourself. No one else can decide whether or not someone wants to overcome their addiction - only the person addicted has this power within them.

Once you understand what is necessary for successful recovery, you must make a firm decision within yourself about committing completely to getting clean and staying clean. No matter what obstacles may arise along the way. Once this decision is made, you must stick by it with every ounce of strength you possess.

****

During our sessions together, I could see that Jack's belief in himself was growing stronger. He made a conscious decision to pursue recovery with all that he had. He was committed to doing whatever it took to overcome his addiction, and he was willing to put in the hard work required for long-term success. Together, we worked on developing coping strategies for triggers and cravings, building a strong support system, and cultivating a positive mindset.

It wasn't always easy. There were times when Jack felt discouraged or overwhelmed, but through it all, he held onto the belief that recovery was possible and that it was possible even for him. In the end, that belief proved to be one of the most powerful tools in his journey toward ending his addiction.

****

Believe Someone Else Believes in YOU

Some find it to be too hard, nearly impossible, to believe that this monumental change is possible for them. I get it... in fact, I have been there. If you end up in this desperate position, find someone who you believe in and who believes in you more than you believe in yourself. This should be someone who believes in you and your ability to change. Maybe they remember you before your addiction and still see a glimmer of that person shining through. Maybe, against impossible odds, they have ended their own addiction. Or maybe they just know how easy change can be when you have the right mindset, possess the right tools, and know that anyone can recover from addiction and do so permanently.

I want you to know that even though I do not know you personally, I believe in you and in your ability to be completely and permanently free from your addiction.

I know that you can do it and I am going to tell you how; what tools to use, how to talk to your doctor, and where to find the help and support you need. I have worked with THOUSANDS of people over the past 30 years who felt they were hopelessly and permanently addicted and who are now living life addiction-free.

****

My Story

Thirty plus years ago, I was one of those who was "hopelessly and permanently addicted." Practically every male I had ever known was addicted to drugs, alcohol, or both. Most also struggled with a variety of

other addictions such as gambling, codependency, violence, pornography, or other addictions. I started my own substance use by age 5, accelerated my use by age 12, and was hopelessly addicted by age 15. By then I had already dropped out of school and fully expected that I would be dead before my 21st birthday. Obviously, God had other plans, and you will read more about that at the end of the chapter.

I became clean and sober more than 30 years ago, and I have remained that way—free from drugs and alcohol and the variety of other addictive tendencies that kept me stuck in destructive patterns.

These patterns kept me from having the life I wanted. I surrendered my will and my life over to the care of God and asked for help. I began a new way of living and decided on a new path that bore no resemblance to the life I was living. I essentially ended my addiction to my old self and created a new self that gave me the outcomes I wanted in my life. I also began to help others in their recovery. I began to live ... to feel pleasure and pain, joy and sadness, to struggle, and to be victorious.

It is so easy to discard the people we see as evil, criminal, stupid, unlovable, addicted, uneducated, lazy, and useless. It is easier to discard them like trash than to try to understand them ... to try to love them ... and to try to see the world the way they see it. It is so much easier to hate them than to love them.

I have been one of the evil, criminal, stupid, unlovable, addicted, uneducated, lazy, useless people and many had discarded me as unredeemable. There was a time in my life when I put myself in places and situations where I could have been shot, attacked, or hurt by someone who was just trying to protect themselves. During my teen years I had been mugged, attacked, beaten unconscious, and had knives and guns pointed at me on numerous occasions. No, I was never dangerous and never really would have hurt anyone. I could certainly see how I could be threatening and if someone had taken a shot at me during one of those times, it would have been my fault. I would have had it coming.

Even many of my family members thought I was useless and worthless and would be best discarded as the trash I presented myself to be. In fact, even though there is not a shred of resemblance left of that person, some of my family still hold that image of me and keep their distance. Even after 30 years, there are still family events I am not invited to. I fully believe that this is because these people still associate me with who I was all those years ago.

Through every moment, even my worst moments, God knew me as His child and believed in me, even when I did not believe in God. I was as valuable to Him at my worst, as I am to Him at my best. God used many human angels to show His love for me, to nurture me, and to redeem me as the Child of the One True King[6] that He always knew me to be. He placed people in my life who never gave up on me. Some believed in me much more than I could possibly believe in myself and pushed me to be the person they saw inside. Praise God and the many people He placed in my life for never giving up on me.

If God never gave up on me, I believe He expects that we are never to give up on each other, even when we are at our worst. Even when we seem scary, dangerous, and so very different from everyone that we know. Dr. Martin Luther King Jr. had a great deal to say about this. He said, "now there is a final reason I think that Jesus says, 'Love your enemies.' It is this: that love has within it a redemptive power. And there is a power there that eventually transforms individuals. Just keep being friendly to that person. Just keep loving

---

[6] MercyMe. (2014). Flawless [Recorded by MercyMe]. On Welcome to the New [MP3]. Fair Trade Services.

them... sometimes they'll hate you a little more at that transition period, but just keep loving them. And by the power of your love they will break down under the load. That's love, you see. It is redemptive, and this is why Jesus says love. There's something about love that builds up and is creative. There is something about hate that tears down and is destructive. So love your enemies." [7]

****

Overcoming an addiction may seem impossible at first glance, but with these three (or four) prerequisites firmly established, there is nothing stopping you from achieving a healthy lifestyle free from addiction!

---

[7] Reference: King Jr., M. L. (2010). Strength to Love. Beacon Press.

SECTION TWO: UNDERSTANDING THE MIND

Chapter 4: The Radical Cause Concept: Taking Responsibility for Your Life

Have you ever found yourself feeling like a victim of your circumstances? Have you ever blamed others for your problems and felt powerless to change them? It's a common experience, but there's a different way of approaching life that can change everything. The Radical Cause Concept is about choosing to see yourself as being at cause for everything in your life, rather than living at the effect of other people.

This doesn't mean that everything is your fault or that you're responsible for other people's actions. It simply means taking full responsibility for your thoughts, feelings, and actions and not allowing others to have control over your identity. By doing so, you become empowered to create the life you want.

Have you ever felt like your life is completely out of your control? That no matter what you do, external circumstances and other people's actions always seem to dictate how you feel and what you do? If so, you are not alone. Many people find themselves living at the effect of others, giving away their power and allowing themselves to become victims of circumstance and other people's desires and expectations.

When you live at the effect of others, you give away your power. You allow external circumstances and other people's actions to determine how you feel and what you do. This can lead to feelings of frustration, helplessness, and resentment. In extreme cases, it can even lead to having access to fewer internal resources and developing a victim mindset that leads one to further victimization and trauma.

Why do you give away your power in this way? There could be many reasons. Perhaps you have been conditioned or programmed from childhood to believe that you have little control over your life. Maybe you have experienced trauma or hardship that has left you feeling powerless. Perhaps you lack the confidence or skills needed to take charge of your own life.

Whatever the reason, it is important to recognize that living at the effect of others, or subconsciously allowing others to dictate the way you live your life, is not a sustainable or healthy way to live. It robs you of your agency and leaves you vulnerable to outside forces beyond your control, essentially setting you up to be a victim of people, circumstances, or history.

What can you do about it? The first step is recognizing that you have a choice in how you respond to external circumstances. You may not be able to control everything that happens around you, but you can control how you think, feel, and act.

The next step is taking ownership of your life. This means setting goals, making plans, and taking action toward those goals regardless of external factors. It means learning new skills and building up your inner resources so that you can weather any storm.

Finally, it means letting go of any victim mentality or self-pity that may be holding you back. Instead, focus on gratitude for what you have and take pride in your accomplishments no matter how small they may seem.

When you choose to take responsibility for your life, everything changes. You become the creator of your reality rather than a victim of it. You start to see opportunities, whereas before you may have only seen obstacles. You begin to take steps toward creating the life you want rather than waiting for someone else to make it happen.

It all starts with a shift in mindset. Instead of blaming others or circumstances for your problems, start looking inward. Take ownership of your thoughts, feelings and actions. Recognize that you have the power to create positive change in your life.

No longer do setbacks or failures feel like insurmountable obstacles. Instead, they become opportunities for growth and learning. You start to see challenges as part of the journey toward achieving your goals rather than roadblocks preventing you from getting there.

Taking responsibility for your life is a path to empowerment. It's about recognizing that you can choose your own destiny and by taking action toward creating the life you want, anything is possible. Embrace the idea that YOU are in control of your own life. Chances are it will take you somewhere amazing!

The radical cause concept also means recognizing that everyone has their own journey and their own challenges. It's not about blaming others or judging them for their actions. One of the key aspects of this idea is that we should not blame others or judge them for their actions. Instead, it's about acknowledging that we all have our own struggles and that we can only control ourselves. This means taking ownership of our choices and decisions and accepting the consequences of those choices. Everyone is doing the best they can with the resources they have.

When you embrace the Radical Cause Concept, you become more mindful of your actions and how they impact others. You start to see yourself as part of a larger community, rather than just an individual pursuing your own goals. You begin to recognize the interconnectedness of all things and how your actions can have ripple effects throughout society.

But this doesn't mean that you should become passive or complacent. On the contrary, it means that you should take an active role in shaping your life and your world. It means being proactive instead of reactive and seeking out opportunities to make positive changes in yourself and in society.

It means recognizing your own agency and power to affect change, rather than simply accepting the status quo. By embracing this mindset, you can become more engaged and passionate about the causes you care about, whether that is social justice, environmentalism, or something else entirely. Rather than feeling powerless in the face of daunting challenges, you can take concrete steps toward creating a better future for yourself and those around you. Ultimately, the Radical Cause Concept is about realizing your own potential as an agent of change in a complex and ever-changing world.

This mindset can be a powerful tool for personal growth and transformation and can help you to recover from your addictions. By adopting this mindset, you'll be able to break free from limiting beliefs and destructive patterns of behavior, allowing you to pursue your goals with greater clarity and purpose. This approach will empower you to take charge of your life, make positive changes, and achieve your full potential.

The Radical Cause Concept can be helpful in addressing addictive behaviors when you take responsibility for your thoughts, feelings, and actions related to addiction. You can begin to identify the underlying causes of your addiction and take steps toward healing.

For example, instead of blaming external factors or other people for your addiction, you can acknowledge that you have control over your choices and take ownership of your recovery journey. You'll also be able to recognize patterns of behavior or thought processes that contribute to your addiction and work toward changing them.

Additionally, by adopting a mindset of personal responsibility, you may feel more empowered to seek out professional help or join support groups that can aid in your recovery process.

The Radical Cause Concept may not provide a cure-all solution for addiction, but it can be a valuable tool in promoting self-awareness and empowering you to take control of your life.

By taking responsibility for your life, you also inspire others to do the same. You become a leader rather than a follower, showing others what is possible when we choose to take ownership of our thoughts, feelings, and actions.

****

I had a client named Sarah who felt like life was just happening to her. She had grown up in difficult circumstances and had always believed that her fate was out of her hands. She worked hard at her job, but never seemed to get ahead. She struggled in relationships and often felt alone and unsupported.

Sarah was stuck in a victim mindset. This way of

thinking had a profound impact on her life and caused her to lose the resources she needed to keep herself safe and secure.

When Sarah was in a relationship, she often felt like the other person held all the power. She would give up her own needs and desires to keep the other person happy, which often led to her feeling taken advantage of or victimized.

Sarah also struggled with setting boundaries at work and in other areas of her life. She would take on too much responsibility or let others walk all over her because she did not feel like she had the power to say no.

This victim mindset caused Sarah to repeatedly end up in situations where she felt helpless and powerless. It seemed like nothing ever went right for her, and she could not understand why.

It was not until Sarah realized that she could take ownership of her life that things began to change. By recognizing that she could choose to do things differently, Sarah was able to start making changes that helped her feel more empowered and in control. She stopped blaming others for her problems and started looking for solutions instead of dwelling on the past. As she gained confidence in herself, Sarah began setting goals for the future.

At first, progress was slow. It seemed like every step forward was met with two steps back. But Sarah refused to give up. She kept pushing herself outside of her comfort zone and seeking out opportunities for growth. Over time, Sarah's mindset shifted from one of victimhood to one of empowerment. She began seeing obstacles as opportunities for growth and change. She started taking risks and making bold moves toward the life she wanted.

As Sarah started taking responsibility for herself, amazing things began to happen. She became more confident in herself. She was promoted at work and started earning more money than ever before. She met someone special who supported her dreams and aspirations. Most importantly, Sarah found a sense of purpose that had been missing from her life before.

****

Chapter 5: Understanding Abraham Maslow's Hierarchy of Needs

When it comes to overcoming addiction, understanding Abraham Maslow's Hierarchy of Needs can be a powerful tool for personal development and self-actualization. The hierarchy states that for individuals to reach their full potential and achieve self-actualization, certain needs must first be met. These include physiological needs, safety and security needs, love and belonging needs, esteem needs, and self-actualization. If basic needs are not met, the hierarchy states, more complex ones cannot be met.

Addiction often stems from unmet needs in one or more areas of the hierarchy. For example, individuals struggling with addiction may use substances to satisfy physiological or emotional needs, such as stress relief or social acceptance. However, this ultimately hinders their ability to progress toward higher-level goals such as personal growth and fulfillment.

Understanding Maslow's Hierarchy of Needs is crucial when it comes to ending addiction because it provides insight into what drives an individual's behavior and where additional motivation might come from. By reflecting on which needs are not being met within the hierarchy, individuals can prioritize those areas more heavily in their journey toward recovery. Additionally, recognizing obstacles between oneself and higher-level goals can help an individual craft more effective solutions while keeping focus on long-term achievement. By meeting lower-level needs first before focusing on higher-level ones, individuals can build a foundation for lasting change in their lives. With persistence and dedication to personal growth, anyone can overcome addiction and achieve their full potential.

Abraham Maslow's Hierarchy of Needs: A Guide to Personal Development and Self-Actualization

When it comes to understanding our journey toward personal development and striving for self-actualization, few concepts are as important as Abraham Maslow's Hierarchy of Needs. Let's explore the concept, why it is so important for personal development, and how best to use this hierarchy on your journey.

What is Maslow's Hierarchy of Needs?

Maslow's Hierarchy of Needs is a psychological theory developed by psychologist Abraham Maslow in the 1940s. The hierarchy states that for an individual to progress toward self-actualization, achieving one's full potential, certain needs must first be met. This includes physiological needs (food, water, shelter), safety/security needs (protection from harm and insecurity), love and belonging needs (relationships with family members, friends, or others), esteem needs (respect from others), and finally self-actualization (the realization of one's full potential).

Maslow argued that these needs form a hierarchy; base-level needs must be fulfilled before higher-level ones can take priority. For example, if an individual does not have their basic physiological needs satisfied, such as having enough food or having adequate shelter, then their ability to experience love and belonging or reach their highest potential will be impaired.

Why Is This Important for Personal Development?

Understanding Maslow's Hierarchy of Needs is essential when it comes to personal development because it provides insight into how individuals prioritize different goals throughout their life. Knowing what type of motivation drives you—whether that be acceptance from peers or achieving a certain accomplishment—can help better orient you on your path to success. Furthermore, understanding where you currently stand in terms of need satisfaction can provide useful insights into where additional motivation might come from. If you are struggling with feelings of loneliness or insecurity, then you may want to prioritize finding sources of community and security to feel a greater sense of fulfillment. Finally, recognizing obstacles between yourself and higher-level goals, such as a lack of resources, will help you craft more effective solutions moving forward while keeping your focus on long-term achievement.

How Can I Use This for My Own Journey?

Using the framework provided by Maslow's hierarchy can be incredibly helpful during your journey toward personal development and self-actualization. First and foremost, take time to reflect on which areas within the hierarchy you currently feel most connected with relative satisfaction levels across each category should become immediately apparent. If there are any particular areas in which you feel lacking—whether it be interpersonal relationships or feeling confident about skills—then make sure these areas get prioritized more heavily than others until improvement has been made. Secondly, keep an eye out for any possible pitfalls that could inhibit growth. If transitioning through stages becomes too difficult then finding alternative paths—mentorships or professional courses—could provide useful assistance along the way. Finally, don't forget to stay motivated; rewards and recognition go a long way in ensuring timely progression while repeated exposure can aid mastery over various topics. Keep an eye out for anything impeding movement up this ladder; neglecting any single aspect could lead to unintended consequences further down the line!

While it's important to have these basic needs met, getting stuck at this level can lead to a skewed perspective on life. When someone is stuck in the safety and security level of Maslow's Hierarchy of Needs, they tend to see everything through the lens of safety and security. Basic needs seem at-risk and unstable, which leads to anxiety and fear.

One major consequence of being stuck at the safety and

security level is that love and belonging in relationships always seem to be threatened. The person may feel like they cannot trust anyone or that everyone is out to get them. They may struggle with forming meaningful relationships because they are too focused on their own survival.

Another consequence is that esteem seems false with impostor syndrome raging. The person may feel like they do not deserve success or recognition for their achievements because they have not yet achieved complete safety and security. This can lead to feelings of inadequacy, low self-esteem, and a lack of confidence in one's abilities.

It is important for individuals who find themselves stuck at the safety and security level to recognize their situation so they can take steps toward breaking free from this trap. One way to do this is by addressing any underlying fears or anxieties that may be holding them back from moving up Maslow's hierarchy.

Therapy can be helpful in identifying these fears, as well as developing practical strategies for overcoming them. Additionally, building healthy relationships with others can help individuals feel more secure in their social connections.

While it is important to prioritize our basic needs for survival, getting stuck at the safety and security level can prevent us from reaching our full potential as human beings. By recognizing this trap and taking active steps toward personal growth, we can break free from its hold on our lives.

Chapter 6: Understanding the Neurological Levels of the Mind

The neurological levels of the mind are an interconnected set of levels from the highest level of our greater self, down to our environment, which forms the base level. Each level affects the levels above and below it, and each level can be changed to affect the other levels. The logical levels of the mind are a change model and provide a useful model to understand ways we can achieve change at an individual and organizational level. The logical levels are: The Greater Self, Identity, Belief, Values, Potential, Behavior, Outcomes, and Environment. You may see other practitioners or organizations with a somewhat different list.

The neurological levels, originally defined by Robert Dilts, are a useful framework for understanding human behavior and personal development. While there may be variations in the list depending on who you ask, when it comes to ending addictions, the focus is often put on the middle levels of identity, belief, values, potential, behavior, and outcomes. These levels are crucial in understanding why addiction manifests and how individuals can overcome it. By examining one's identity and beliefs about themselves and their addiction, as well as their values and potential for growth and change, individuals can work toward changing their behaviors and achieving positive outcomes.

The Higher/Greater Self or Purpose

Have you ever wondered why you are here? What is your higher purpose and the greater vision for your life? This is what we call the higher or greater self or purpose, which encompasses the overall sense of purpose and direction in life.

Your greater self is the highest level of your mind which feeds who you are, what you believe in, and what you want to achieve. It defines your one true identity and guides you toward fulfilling your potential.

However, discovering your purpose in life may take years and can be a challenging process. For most people, this question may be difficult to answer since they have never thought about their role in the wider world.

If you have different interests and passions, it may also be hard to figure out your purpose. You might feel lost and not know where to start. But don't worry; feeling lost on this journey is natural.

It takes time, effort, and sacrifices to find your purpose. It is a journey of self-discovery where you follow your own unique path. Remember that most people never find their purpose because they are not even trying.

Start by exploring different areas that interest you and reflect on how they align with your values. With persistence, clarity will come as you discover more about yourself and what truly matters to you.

I have worked with many clients trying to find purpose in life and identify what the higher self meant to them. Let me tell you about three individuals with whom I have worked who were all searching for something more in their lives. One found their path through a deep relationship with God, another found it through a supportive self-help community, and the third found it through a career of helping others.

The first person had always been drawn to spirituality and religion, but it wasn't until he developed a strong relationship with God that he truly found his higher self. Through prayer, meditation, and Bible studies, he was able to connect with something greater than himself and find meaning in his life.

The second person struggled with feelings of isolation and loneliness until she discovered a supportive self-help community through a 12-step program. She joined groups that shared similar interests and values, attended events where she could meet new people, and volunteered for causes that aligned with her beliefs. Through these connections, she found purpose and belonging.

The third person had always felt called to help others but was not sure how to turn that passion into a career. Eventually, he discovered opportunities to work as a Peer Support Professional where he could make a tangible impact on people's lives. By dedicating himself to serving others, he found fulfillment in his work and purpose in his life.

In the end, each person found their own unique path toward discovering their higher self. Whether it was through faith, community support, or helping others - each individual was able to connect with something greater than themselves and find meaning in their life's journey.

Identity

Identity is the level of the mind where you define who

you are as an individual. It is shaped by your beliefs, values, and perceptions of yourself. This level of the mind also establishes your relationship with the outside world and how you view yourself in relation to others.

You probably often identify yourself with different areas of your life, such as your job/career/education, role at work, within the family, or in romantic relationships. For example, if someone asked you, "Who are you?" you may reply, "I am a physician."

Knowing who you are is crucial to living an authentic life. Self-awareness is key in understanding yourself, and is shaped by your experiences and the choices you make. Identity formation is a matter of "finding oneself." The complex question of "Who am I?" needs an in-depth exploration of your talents and potential with available social roles.

Your identity is what defines you as a person. It encompasses memories, experiences, self-esteem, and self-worth. It's something that is malleable and develops as you confront challenges and grow in life.

Having a strong sense of identity leads to a happier and more fulfilled life. So, take time to reflect on who you are —explore your interests and passions, understand your values and beliefs, and embrace your unique qualities.

****

Several years ago, I had a client, a young woman named Emily, who felt lost and uncertain about her life's direction. She was very early in her recovery from addictive relationships and was determined not to fall into the same old patterns. She had always followed the expectations of her family and friends, but she couldn't shake the feeling that there was more to life than finding a nice man who would take care of her.

Emily decided to take a step back from dating and her busy life and reflect on what truly mattered to her. She started journaling every day, writing down her thoughts and feelings without any judgment or hesitation.

As she continued to write, Emily began to uncover parts of herself that she had never explored before. She discovered a passion for painting and started taking art classes. She realized that helping others brought her immense joy and started volunteering to help younger students with art classes.

Through this process of self-reflection and exploration, Emily learned more about what she valued, her core beliefs, and who she truly was as a person. She understood that her identity was not just defined by external factors like her job or relationships, but also by her innermost desires, values, and beliefs.

With this newfound self-awareness, Emily made choices that aligned with her true self. She eventually quit her job in finance to pursue a career in art therapy, which combined both of her passions. She surrounded herself with people who supported and encouraged her authentic self and stopped worrying about those who passed judgement on her following her dreams and having the life she truly desired.

Though it was not always easy, Emily felt more fulfilled than ever before. By getting to know herself deeply, she was able to live an authentic life full of purpose and meaning.

****

Beliefs

This is the level of the mind where you define what you believe in and consider to be true. These beliefs shape the way you think, feel, and act. This level of the mind flows from the values that you hold and the standards by which you operate.

Everyone has a personal belief system that defines how they see and interact with the world. Many of our beliefs have been handed down to us from our family. Sometimes they are installed in us by our heritage, nationality, or other factors. Our beliefs are our beliefs and we believe them simply because we believe them ... often very little thought or analysis has been imparted and often we have faulty or limiting beliefs.

When your thoughts, feelings, and actions are in congruence with your personal beliefs, you experience a sense of satisfaction and contentment.

Your beliefs can also be influenced by the media you consume and the messages you receive from society. For instance, if you are constantly exposed to images of thin models on social media or in advertising campaigns, this may influence your beliefs about body image and what constitutes physical attractiveness.

For example, someone who grew up in a conservative family may hold the belief that traditional gender roles are essential in a household. This belief could have been passed down to them by their parents or grandparents and reinforced throughout their upbringing. As a result, they may feel uncomfortable with the idea of women working outside of the home or men taking on domestic responsibilities. However, if this individual's thoughts, feelings, and actions align with this belief system, they may experience a sense of satisfaction and contentment. Conversely, if they were to challenge this belief and act in opposition to it, they may experience cognitive dissonance and discomfort. In either case, personal beliefs play a significant role in shaping one's worldview and experiences.

Another example could be someone who holds the belief that hard work and perseverance are the keys to success. This belief may have been instilled in them by their parents or through experiences of working hard to achieve their goals. As a result, they may feel motivated to put in long hours and make sacrifices to reach their desired outcomes. When their thoughts, feelings, and actions align with this belief system, they may experience a sense of pride and accomplishment when they achieve their goals. If they were to encounter setbacks or obstacles despite their hard work, it may challenge this belief system and cause them to question its validity. Someone holding the belief that success is solely based on hard work and perseverance could lead them to believe that any success achieved without those qualities is not truly earned or deserved. This can create a rigid mindset where they feel like they must constantly work hard and put in long hours to be considered successful. As a result, they may neglect other important aspects of their life such as their mental and physical health, relationships, and leisure time.

It is important to recognize that while your beliefs are shaped by these kinds of external factors, you also have the power to examine and challenge them. By becoming more aware of where your beliefs come from and how they impact your thoughts and actions, you can begin to make conscious choices about which beliefs serve you best.

Values

This is the level of the mind where you determine what is important to you. Your values form the basis of your decision-making process and influence your behavior. This level of the mind is also where you establish the goals and objectives that you are striving to achieve.

Your values play a crucial role in shaping your identity and beliefs. These values act as guiding principles for decision-making and behavior, influencing how you interact with the world around you. The level of the mind where you define what you believe to be true and valuable is deeply rooted in your values and standards. This level of the mind shapes your thoughts, feelings, and actions, ultimately contributing to your identity and worldview. Therefore, your values are an integral part of who you are and significantly impact your beliefs about yourself and the world.

There are many common and deeply held values that are shared across cultures and societies. Some of these values include:

- Honesty: being truthful and transparent in all

interactions with others
- Respect: treating others with dignity, empathy, and consideration
- Responsibility: taking ownership of one's actions and being accountable for the consequences
- Integrity: adhering to a set of ethical principles even when faced with challenges or temptations
- Compassion: showing kindness, understanding, and support toward others who are suffering or struggling
- Equality: treating all individuals fairly and without prejudice or discrimination based on factors such as race, gender, religion, or social status
- Freedom: having individual autonomy and independence, including the right to express oneself freely and make choices that align with one's personal values
- Loyalty: demonstrating commitment to family, friends, organizations or communities through unwavering support and dedication
- Courage: facing difficult situations or obstacles with bravery and determination
- Justice: promoting fairness and equality by upholding laws that protect individual rights while ensuring accountability for wrongdoing

These values can vary depending on cultural context but are often seen as universal human values that guide our behavior toward ourselves and others.

Values are the fundamental beliefs you hold dear that govern your life and feed into your beliefs. You need to take a deep look inside yourself to understand your core values. Being in alignment with your personal values makes all the difference in the way you live and work. When your choices and actions are incongruent to your set of values, you may feel internal stress and conflict. This is often a source of frustration and profound unhappiness.

Other common personal core values are achievement, community, love, and family. Identifying and understanding your core values is a challenging exercise for many people. Being aware of what you value most is important and worth your time. When you understand and honor your personal values, it is easier to make crucial decisions. You are guided by a moral compass in decision-making to determine the best direction for you and your life goals.

Values elicitation is a process of identifying and clarifying an individual's core values through structured questioning and reflection. This process can help individuals become more aware of their beliefs, priorities, and motivations, which can inform their decision-making and behavior.

Values elicitation typically involves asking open-ended questions that encourage individuals to reflect on their experiences, preferences, and aspirations. For example, questions may include:

- What do you consider to be the most important things in life?
- What motivates you to take action or make decisions?
- What qualities do you admire in others?
- When have you felt the most fulfilled or satisfied?
- What is important to you about that?
- What will having that provide for you?

Through these types of questions, individuals are encouraged to explore their thoughts and feelings about different aspects of their lives. As they reflect on their responses, patterns may emerge that reveal underlying values.

Values elicitation will usually also involve ranking exercises where individuals prioritize values based on what is most important to them. This can provide further insight into an individual's value hierarchy and help them identify areas where there may be conflicts or trade-offs between competing values.

Overall, values elicitation can be a useful tool for identifying core values by providing a structured framework for self-reflection and exploration. By becoming more aware of your values, you can make more intentional choices aligned with what matters most to you.

Potential

Your neurobiology dictates that you have unlimited potential. This is the level of the mind where you recognize and maximize your potential. It is also where you develop the skills and capabilities necessary to achieve success, set expectations for yourself, and strive to meet those expectations.

Your Unlimited Potential

Your brain is an incredibly complex and incredibly powerful organ, and it can be trained and shaped in almost any way you choose. You can learn, remember, and process information, create and innovate, and even change your behavior and responses to external stimuli. Your ability to adapt and grow is almost limitless, and your potential is only limited by your own imagination and perseverance.

What is your body made of? Your first thought might be that it is made up of different organs—such as your heart, lungs, and stomach—that work together to keep your body going. You might zoom in a level and say your body is made up of many different types of cells. However, at the most basic level, your body—and, in fact, all of life, as well as the nonliving world—is made up of atoms, often organized into larger structures called molecules.

Atoms and molecules follow the rules of chemistry and physics, even when they're part of a complex, living, breathing being. If you learned in chemistry that some atoms tend to gain or lose electrons or form bonds with each other, those facts remain true even when the atoms or molecules are part of a living thing. In fact, simple interactions between atoms—played out many times and in many different combinations, in a single cell or a larger organism—are what make life possible. One could argue that everything you are, including your consciousness, is the byproduct of chemical and electrical interactions between a very, very large number of nonliving atoms!

An atom is the smallest unit of matter that retains all of

the chemical properties of an element. Most of the volume of an atom—greater than 99.99999 percent—is actually empty space. I like to think of this empty space as energy or potential.

Every cell in the body is bathed in neurotransmitters creating a powerful mind-body connection where the body becomes the mind and the mind becomes the body. We used to believe that brain neurotransmitters were to be regarded as belonging ONLY to the brain and nowhere else. We now know that there are more neurotransmitters in our gut than in our brains. In addition, there are clusters of neurotransmitters, or energy centers, located throughout the body. Neurotransmitters bathe every cell in the body, therefore every cell/organ/bone in your body is listening to every thought. Einstein showed us that energy has a direct relationship with matter; energy is latent matter and obviously affects matter. Conversely, matter is condensed energy.

There are an astounding number of neurological connections in the human body. To be precise, there are 10 to the 10th power to the 11th power connections - that's 10 billion written eleven times! These connections allow for communication between neurons and ultimately enable us to function as complex beings. Even the simplest of tasks involves a vast network of these connections working in harmony. It's truly remarkable to consider just how intricate and complex our bodies are on a microscopic level.

The vast number of neurological connections in the human body is indeed scientific evidence of the mind/body connection. These connections allow for communication between the brain and other systems in our bodies, such as the nervous system, endocrine system, and immune system. This means that our thoughts, emotions, and mental states can have a direct impact on our physical health and well-being. It's fascinating to think about how interconnected our minds and bodies truly are, and how important it is to prioritize both aspects of our health so we can live a balanced life.

It is certainly true that the mind and body are intimately connected to the point where they could be seen as one entity rather than two separate things. Our thoughts, emotions, and mental states can have a direct impact on our physical health and well-being, while physical sensations can also affect our mental state. This is why practices such as meditation and mindfulness, which focus on both the mind and body, can have such powerful effects on our overall health. Ultimately, it is important to view ourselves holistically - as whole beings made up of interconnected systems - in order to truly understand and optimize our health and well-being.

Behavior

This is the level of the mind where you take action and put your plans into motion, and where you take risks and strive to achieve your goals. This level of the mind is also where you manage the consequences of your decisions and actions. Who you are is made up of how you think, feel, and act.

Adopting a new habit or breaking an old one is notoriously hard. Human beings generally do not like change. We stick to old routines for various reasons that may include fear of the unknown or fear of failure. What could we achieve if we could overcome these fears and harness the power of behavior to achieve our goals and become the best version of ourselves?

The first step in harnessing the power of behavior is to identify your goals. Whether it is ending an addiction, losing weight, or learning a new skill, knowing what you want to achieve will help you stay focused and motivated.

Next, create a plan to achieve your goals. Break down

your goal into smaller, achievable steps that you can work on each day. Once you have a plan in place, it's time to take action. This is where behavior comes into play. Instead of thinking about making a change or achieving your goal, start acting on it every day. Even small actions can lead to big results over time.

Of course, adopting new habits or breaking old ones is not easy. There will be days when you do not want to stick to your plan or when you slip and make a mistake. Remember that setbacks are a natural part of the process. Do not let them discourage you from continuing your journey.

One way to stay motivated is by tracking your progress. Use a journal or an app to record your daily actions and measure how far you have come toward achieving your goal. In addition, surround yourself with positive influences who support your efforts toward change. Seek out friends or family members who have similar goals or interests as you and join online communities for extra support.

Behavior is a powerful tool that can help you achieve your goals and become better versions of yourself. When you use the steps mentioned above, you'll be able to break free from addictive patterns and embrace the positive changes you're making in your life.

Outcomes

When we talk about outcomes, it is important to understand how they are linked to the neurological levels of the mind. This is where we measure the results of our efforts and reflect on what we have achieved. It is also where we develop skills and strategies to achieve even better outcomes.

Success is not just about setting goals and working hard to achieve them. It is also about reflecting on your achievements and determining what changes need to be made. This is where the outcomes level comes in.

The outcomes level is where you assess and reflect on what you have achieved—both the successes and failures—and determine what changes need to be made going forward. This level of the mind is critical in achieving success because it allows you to develop the necessary skills and strategies needed to achieve even better results.

When you focus solely on setting goals and working hard toward them without taking time to reflect on your progress, you risk missing out on important insights that could help improve your performance. By regularly assessing your outcomes, you can identify areas for improvement, celebrate successes, and adjust course as needed.

If you find that the outcomes you are getting are not what you desire, it is important to take a step back and reflect on your thinking, feeling, and behavior. These three factors play a significant role in determining the outcomes you experience in life.

For example, if you're constantly experiencing negative outcomes such as failed relationships or financial struggles, it may be time to examine your thinking patterns. Are you constantly thinking negatively about yourself or others? Are you stuck in limiting beliefs that prevent you from moving toward your goals? By identifying these patterns and working to shift them, you can create more positive outcomes for yourself.

Similarly, your feelings and behaviors also impact the outcomes you experience. If you are consistently engaging in self-sabotaging behaviors such as procrastination or impulsivity, it is likely that your outcomes will reflect this. By working to change these behaviors and replacing them with more productive habits, you can set yourself up for success.

Ending addiction requires significant changes in thinking, feeling, and behavior. Addiction can be seen as a negative outcome that results from the interplay of these three factors. To overcome addiction, it's essential to address each of these areas.

Firstly, changing thinking patterns is crucial in ending addiction. You may have negative self-talk and limiting beliefs that fuel your addictive behavior. By working to identify and shift these patterns, you can begin to develop a more positive mindset that supports recovery.

Secondly, addressing emotions is also an important part of ending addiction. Many people turn to drugs or alcohol as a way of coping with difficult emotions such as anxiety or depression. If this is true for you, learning healthier ways of managing your emotions and building emotional resilience through techniques like mindfulness can help you reduce your reliance on substances.

Finally, changing behaviors is critical in ending addiction. This includes both stopping addictive behaviors and replacing them with healthier habits. For example, if you struggle with alcohol addiction, you may need to stop drinking entirely while also developing new hobbies or social connections that support sobriety.

Environment

The external environment influences your behavior,

your beliefs, your values, and your potential. This is the level of the mind where you interact with your environment. Very often, either you control your environment, or your environment controls you.

Creating a supportive environment is crucial for you when you are trying to end addiction. This can involve removing triggers and cues that lead to drug or alcohol use, such as avoiding certain people or places associated with substance abuse. It can also mean establishing new routines and habits that support recovery, such as practicing mindfulness or engaging in physical exercise.

By setting up the best possible conditions in your environment, you can increase your chances of success and make it easier to maintain sobriety over time. In addition, seeking out support from friends, family members, or addiction treatment providers can also be an important part of creating a positive and supportive environment for ending addiction.

The environment you choose to spend time in can have a significant impact on your behavior and habits. If you consistently spend time in a place where alcohol is present, such as a bar or nightclub, it's more likely that you will be tempted to drink. Conversely, if you spend time in an environment where physical activity is encouraged, such as a gym or fitness class, you are more likely to engage in exercise and make it a regular part of your routine. This is why it's important to be intentional about the environments you choose to spend time in and to create conditions that support the behaviors and habits you want to adopt.

Environment encompasses everything outside of yourself and that are a result of the self. It is the state of the external context where people live. Your surroundings influence your thoughts, feelings and actions every day. Recognizing the impact of the environment on your well-being is vital.

Putting it all together

Being conscious of the neurological logical levels of the mind can help you understand at what level you are attempting to make change. Sometimes, you might waste time trying to make change at a lower level when you need to consider a higher hierarchical level to achieve that change. If you want to achieve a desired change in life, think about the logical level at which you are operating.

You need to be aware of limiting beliefs and the values that feed those beliefs if you are to change the self. Moreso, you need to understand the great and unlimited potential within yourself and around you so that you can create a new reality.

You must believe that change is possible, that change is possible for you, and that you are deciding right now that you want this change and are willing to do what is needed to have this change.

Chapter 7: End Addiction by Shifting Thinking Using Psycho-Cybernetics

The idea of being trapped in an unhealthy cycle of addiction is daunting and hard to break free from. With the right approach, you can use psycho-cybernetics to help shift your thinking so that you can break out of the addiction. Developed by Dr. Maxwell Maltz, psycho-cybernetics is a self-improvement technique that helps people change their thought patterns and beliefs to achieve their goals.

It is a holistic system for self-improvement that draws from psychology and cybernetics - the science of control and communication. This philosophy suggests that our minds are like supercomputers, constantly taking in information, processing it, and forming beliefs about ourselves as a result. This results in programming that starts at the moment of conception and may even occur generationally, and it continues throughout our lifespan. However, if at any point we decide we do not like the outcomes of that programming, we can 'reprogram' our brains to make better decisions and move closer toward our goals.

Many of us have faulty thought patterns and maladaptive feedback mechanisms. We've been programmed with negative beliefs about ourselves and our abilities that hold us back from achieving what we want. Psycho-cybernetics seeks to correct these faulty mechanisms by reprogramming the subconscious mind.

There are four steps to using psycho-cybernetics to improve your life:

1. Define your goal
   The first step is to clearly define what it is that you want. This could be anything from losing weight to starting a business to ending an addiction.
2. Visualize success
   Next, visualize yourself achieving your goal in vivid detail. See yourself as if you've already achieved it.
3. Develop positive habits
   To reinforce this new self-image, develop positive habits that align with your goal.
4. Use feedback loops

Finally, use feedback loops to continually adjust your behavior until you achieve your desired outcome. Just as a missile can use feedback mechanisms to correct its course and hit its target, our brains can use feedback loops to guide us toward our goals.

So how can you apply psycho-cybernetics in your own life? Here are a few tips:

1. Identify limiting beliefs
   Take some time to identify any negative beliefs you have about yourself or your abilities. Identifying limiting beliefs can be a challenging but important process in personal growth. When you notice yourself saying things like "I could never do that" or "I'm not good enough," take note of it.
2. Replace negative thoughts with positive thoughts
   Whenever you catch yourself thinking negatively, replace those thoughts with positive affirmations. Replacing negative thoughts with positive affirmations can be a powerful tool for overcoming limiting beliefs and achieving personal growth. Repeating your positive affirmations often is key to reinforcing new neural pathways in

your brain that support your new beliefs about yourself.

3. Visualize success

   Spend time each day visualizing yourself achieving your goals in vivid detail. The first step is to set clear goals for yourself. Make sure they are specific, measurable, achievable, relevant, and time-bound (SMART). Close your eyes and imagine yourself achieving your goal in as much detail as possible. Visualize every aspect of the experience - what it looks like, feels like, sounds like, smells like. Engage all your senses when visualizing success. For example, if your goal is to run a marathon, visualize the feel of the pavement beneath your feet, the sound of the crowd cheering you on, and the taste of victory at the finish line.

4. Develop positive habits

   Developing positive habits is an important key to creating lasting change in your life. Start with small changes that are easy to implement and build up from there. Remember that developing positive habits takes time and effort, but it's worth it in the end! By creating daily habits that support your new self-image and move you closer toward your goals, you can create lasting change in your life and achieve even more than you thought possible.

5. Use feedback loops

    Using feedback loops is a powerful way to continually evaluate your progress and adjust your behavior as needed until you achieve the results you desire. Define metrics that will help you measure your progress toward your goals. Remember that feedback loops are an ongoing process; it's important to continually evaluate and adjust until you achieve success! By using feedback loops to track progress toward clear goals, you can stay focused on what matters most and make continuous improvements along the way.

One way that psycho-cybernetics helps with addiction is by changing our perspectives. We are often drawn toward certain things because they bring us comfort or pleasure, but those same things might be unhealthy for us in certain cases. By recognizing this dynamic, we can start making more conscious choices, rather than giving in to impulses that ruin our well-being in the long run.

Another way that psycho-cybernetics can help us with addictions is by recognizing our weaknesses as well as our strengths. Many people who struggle with various addictions may have a tendency to belittle themselves or give up at times when faced with challenges; however, through using this system, individuals can start viewing their 'weaknesses' as potentials for growth instead of failure points. By regularly practicing visualization techniques, such as picturing success and picturing where you want to be one year from now - we can motivate ourselves to stay on track despite any obstacles we face along the way.

Finally, psycho-cybernetic principles allow us to recognize patterns within ourselves and learn how best to respond when confronted with triggers or situations which encourage unwanted behaviors. Realizing these patterns helps us build healthier habits by allowing us to take control of what we do when faced with cravings and temptations which may otherwise pull us down. By developing an understanding of why certain behaviors occur and replacing them with healthier alternatives, individuals will have much more success in overcoming their mental vice than if they simply deny its existence altogether!

Addiction often stems from deep-seated emotional issues, such as stress, anxiety, or trauma. These emotions can trigger negative thought patterns that lead to addictive behaviors. By using psycho-cybernetics techniques such as visualization and positive affirmations, individuals can reprogram their subconscious mind to break free from these negative thought patterns. This can help them overcome cravings and reduce the likelihood of relapse. For example, an individual struggling with alcohol addiction may visualize themselves as healthy and sober while repeating positive affirmations such as "I am in control of my choices" or "I am capable of overcoming this addiction." This type of visualization helps shift their focus away from the addiction itself and toward a healthier future.

Overall, Psycho-cybernetics can be an incredibly powerful tool to aid individuals in shifting their thinking patterns so that they can overcome addictions. However, for the approach to be most effective you should seek out the assistance of a skilled practitioner who specializes in addiction recovery.

SECTION THREE: UNDERSTANDING ADDICTION INTERVENTIONS

Chapter 8: Taking Responsibility for Your Own Addiction Recovery

Addictions can be difficult to overcome without the right support, but taking responsibility for your own addiction recovery is a powerful step forward. By admitting that you have an addiction and committing to finding help, you can move in the direction of healing and eventually end your addiction. Taking ownership of your addiction recovery process means recognizing that only you can decide when it's time to seek help and build the life you always wanted.

Once you've made that decision, there are many things you can do to get started.

First, talk to people who have recovered from addictions themselves or work with a practitioner who understands the underlying causes of addiction. This will help give you a better understanding of why you have an addiction in the first place and what steps are needed to end it.

Once you have enough knowledge about your condition, make an action plan that outlines specific strategies for ending your addiction and conquering your cravings. For example, your plan could include a daily journaling practice designed around your triggers, as well as activities such as EFT (Emotional Freedom Techniques) and self-hypnosis, which will help reduce stress levels.

Whether it's drugs, alcohol, gambling, or any other addictive behavior, breaking free from addiction requires a comprehensive approach that addresses the social, physical, emotional, mental, and spiritual aspects of your life.

Developing an action plan to take responsibility for ending your addiction can be a daunting task. However, with commitment and dedication, you can create a roadmap for recovery that includes strategies to address each dimension of your life.

Social Approach

Social support is crucial when it comes to overcoming addiction. Surrounding yourself with people who encourage and motivate you can help you stay on track. Consider joining a support group or attending counseling sessions where you can connect with others who are going through similar experiences.

Physical Approach

The physical aspect of addiction is often overlooked but plays a significant role in recovery. Engaging in regular exercise improves overall health and helps to alleviate stress and anxiety associated with withdrawal symptoms. Additionally, adopting healthy eating habits and getting enough sleep can aid in the recovery process.

Emotional Approach

Emotional regulation is essential when it comes to managing addiction. Developing coping mechanisms such as mindfulness meditation or deep breathing exercises can help regulate emotions during stressful situations. It may also be beneficial to seek out therapy to work through underlying emotional issues that contribute to addictive behaviors.

Mental Approach

Many individuals struggling with addiction have negative thought patterns that perpetuate their behavior. Addressing these thoughts head-on through brain training or other forms of talk therapy can help shift negative thinking patterns into more positive ones.

Spiritual Approach

Lastly, addressing the spiritual component of addiction involves finding meaning and purpose beyond the addictive behavior. This could involve engaging in activities such as volunteering or practicing gratitude daily.

Developing an action plan that incorporates social, physical, emotional, mental, and spiritual approaches is key when taking responsibility for ending addiction. Remember that recovery is a journey and may involve setbacks along the way. However, committing yourself to this holistic approach toward healing, both physically and mentally, will ultimately lead you toward lasting change in your life!

Finally, do not be afraid to ask for help if needed. There are plenty of resources that specialize in helping those struggling with addiction find support.

By taking responsibility for your own addiction recovery process, you will gain greater control over your life while also building resilience along the way. This doesn't mean that recovering from an addiction will be easy—it will take hard work and dedication—but by embracing this challenge head on and seeking professional assistance where necessary, it is possible to create a healthier life free from addictive behaviors.

Here are some examples of how taking responsibility can create positive changes in an individual's life:

- Improved Relationships
  When you take responsibility for your actions and choices, it becomes easier to communicate effectively with others. You're less likely to blame them for problems and more likely to work together to find solutions. This can lead to stronger, healthier relationships with family, friends, and colleagues.
- Increased Confidence
  Taking ownership of your life means believing in yourself and your ability to create the life you want. This confidence can spill over into other areas of your life, such as work or hobbies, leading to increased success and fulfillment.
- Better Health
  When you take responsibility for your health, you are more likely to make healthy choices like eating well and exercising regularly. This can lead to improved physical health and mental well-being.

- Career Advancement
  Taking ownership of your career means setting goals, developing skills, and seeking out opportunities for growth. This can lead to promotions or new job opportunities that align with your passions and values.
- Greater Happiness
  Ultimately, taking ownership of your life leads to greater happiness and fulfillment. When we feel like we are in control of our lives and making progress toward our goals, we experience a sense of purpose and satisfaction that is hard to come by otherwise.

These are just a few examples. There are countless ways that taking ownership can positively impact an individual's life!

Chapter 9: Ending Addiction Through Mindfulness Practice

Mindfulness can be a powerful tool for those looking to end an addiction. By focusing your attention on the present moment, you can become aware of your own thoughts, feelings, and behavior patterns. This can help you to gain clarity about the source(s) of your addiction, and to develop healthier ways of responding to them. Additionally, achieving a positive mindset through mindfulness can help reduce stress levels, increase self-awareness, and facilitate long-term change.

If you're trying to end an addiction, start by learning what mindfulness is and how to become more aware of your thoughts. This could include setting aside time each day for meditation or simply taking deep breaths to focus on the present moment. Once you've become comfortable with the basics of mindfulness, try implementing some more advanced techniques, such as being honest about your emotions or accepting them without attempting to control them. Additionally, when it comes to addiction recovery, challenging the negative thought patterns that often accompany addictions is important for maintaining a positive mindset. Ask yourself if those thoughts are truly helping or hindering progress toward ending your addiction.

In addition to improving mental clarity and reducing stress levels, practicing mindfulness can also help establish healthy boundaries when it comes to addictive behaviors. Rather than trying to hide or ignore these impulses entirely, recognize when they're occurring without judgment or shame so that they don't continue unchecked. Doing so will enable you to respond differently in the future by either choosing not to engage in certain activities that may lead you down a destructive path or finding other ways of addressing them such as therapy or joining a support group.

Using Mindfulness to End an Addiction: 10 Practices for Recovery

Addiction is a complex issue that affects millions of people worldwide. Many individuals try to overcome their addiction through traditional methods such as therapy, medication, or rehab. While these approaches can be effective, they may not address the underlying causes of addiction.

Mindfulness has emerged as a powerful tool in addiction recovery. By focusing on the present moment and accepting one's thoughts and emotions without judgment, mindfulness can help individuals break free from destructive patterns and build healthier habits.

Here are ten different mindfulness practices that can support addiction recovery:

1. Breathing Exercises

Conscious breathing techniques such as 4-5-6 breathing, diaphragmatic breathing, alternate nostril breathing, or square breathing can help you regulate your emotions and reduce stress levels. These exercises promote relaxation and increase oxygen flow to the brain, which can improve focus and clarity.

> Example: Sit comfortably with your back straight and your eyes closed. Inhale deeply through your nose for four seconds, hold your breath for two seconds, then exhale slowly through your mouth for six seconds. Repeat this pattern for several minutes.

2. Body Scan Meditation

Body scan meditation involves mentally scanning each part of the body, paying attention to any sensations or discomforts without trying to change them. This practice promotes physical awareness and can help you connect with your body in a non-judgmental way.

> Example: Lie down on your back with your arms by your side and close your eyes. Starting from the top of your head, scan down through each part of the body (face, neck, shoulders, etc.), noticing any sensations you feel along the way without trying to change them.

3. Loving-Kindness Meditation

Loving-kindness meditation is a practice that cultivates feelings of compassion toward yourself and others. This technique can help you to develop positive self-esteem and empathy toward others while reducing negative emotions like anger or resentment.

> Example: Sit comfortably with your eyes closed and recall someone who you love unconditionally (a pet or someone dear). Visualize them in front of you and silently repeat phrases like "May you be happy," "May you be healthy," "May you be safe," etc., extending these wishes to yourself then gradually expanding it outwards.

4. Mindful Walking

Mindful walking involves paying attention to each step taken during a walk while remaining fully present in the moment. This practice can help you reconnect with nature while reducing stress levels and improving mood.

> Example: Find a quiet outdoor space where you will not be disturbed (preferably near trees or greenery). Begin walking at a slow pace; take note of how each foot touches the ground - heel first..., How it feels underfoot - soft soil..., What sounds do you hear? Focus on every aspect of walking mindfully until you reach the end point.

5. Gratitude Practice

Gratitude practice involves reflecting on things you are grateful for in life. This cultivates positive emotions like joy or contentment while shifting away from negative ones such as fear or sadness.

> Example: Take some time before bed (or after waking up) to write down three things that happened during the day that made you feel grateful; it could be something as simple as having food on the table or spending time with loved ones.

6. Mindful Eating

Mindful eating involves paying attention to every aspect of eating. Slowing down while eating, chewing your food fully, and savoring flavors can help you to develop a healthier relationship with food by becoming more aware of hunger cues and satiety signals.

> Example: Choose a food item (a fruit, vegetable, etc.) and sit quietly at a table where there are no distractions around... TV off, phone put away, nobody else present, etc. Take note of the color and texture before taking small bites; chew slowly while savoring its flavor before swallowing each bite.

7. Yoga Practice

Yoga incorporates physical postures with breath work & meditation practices; it promotes muscle flexibility & strength whilst calming anxiety-inducing thoughts.

> Example: Sign up for an online yoga class suited for beginners; find comfortable clothing suitable for stretching movements & set aside at least thirty minutes daily for practice.

8. Mindful Journaling

Journaling allows you to express your thoughts freely without fear of judgement; this technique helps you increase self-awareness by identifying triggers that lead you into addictive behaviors.

> Example: Set aside some time

daily/weekly/monthly depending on personal preference & write about experiences/thoughts/feelings encountered throughout those periods.

9. Mindful Communication

Mindful communication involves being present during conversations - listening actively without interrupting, and speaking truthfully without judgment/criticism.

> Example: When engaged in conversation, listen attentively without premeditating responses; give full attention whilst maintaining eye contact; respond truthfully but respectfully.

10. Mindful Visualization

Mindful visualization involves using mental imagery to create a positive outcome or experience in your mind. This technique can help you to overcome negative emotions, anxiety, and stress by shifting your focus toward more positive thoughts and feelings. Mindful visualization can also be used to visualize yourself overcoming addiction and living a healthier life. By creating a clear mental image of what you want to achieve, you can increase motivation and focus on achieving your goals.

> Example: Find a quiet place where you won't be

disturbed and sit comfortably with your eyes closed. Visualize a peaceful scene like a beach, forest, or mountain top. Imagine yourself in this setting; feel the warmth of the sun on your skin, the sound of waves crashing on the shore, or birds chirping in the trees. Take deep breaths and allow yourself to relax into this visualization for several minutes.

Overall, these ten mindfulness practices provide concrete examples of how mindfulness can impact addiction recovery. By incorporating these practices into daily life, you can cultivate greater self-awareness, develop healthier habits, and build resilience against relapse triggers.

Ultimately, mindfulness is just one tool that can be used during addiction recovery, but it has proven to be effective in shifting negative mindsets toward ending an addiction while also providing valuable insight into thoughts and behaviors. With practice and dedication over time, you can use this technique to achieve greater emotional wellbeing and begin creating lasting change within yourself.

Chapter 10: Techniques for Managing Negative Thoughts and Emotions

By reframing your thoughts and beliefs about addiction, you can gain a fresh perspective and find new ways to move forward. Reframing isn't just about positive thinking; it's about creating new neural pathways in your brain that allow you to see things differently. Over time, these new pathways become stronger than the old ones associated with addictive behavior.

Creating new neural pathways is like blazing new paths in the wilderness. Just as a hiker has to cut through the thick undergrowth, battle steep inclines, and navigate his way through treacherous terrain, creating new neural pathways can also be an arduous task. It requires effort and persistence to forge a new path in the brain by practicing new skills or habits. The more frequently you traverse these new pathways, the stronger they become. Just like a well-trodden trail in the woods, over time, these new neural connections become automatic and ingrained, making it easier to access these pathways in the future.

Reframing is a technique used in psychology that involves looking at a situation from a different angle or changing the meaning attached to a situation. By doing this, you can change your emotional response and create new neural pathways for action. When applied to addiction, reframing can help you regain control over your life and end your addictive behaviors.

Instead of looking at addiction as a "losing battle," something that is out of your control, or even predestined by genetics, you can reframe it as a challenge that you choose to face and defeat. When you do this, you shift your focus from feeling helpless to feeling empowered. This shift in mindset can make all the difference when it comes to overcoming addiction.

In addition to reframing addiction itself, you can also reframe the triggers and situations that lead you down the path of addictive behavior. For example, instead of seeing stress as something negative that must be avoided at all costs, you can reframe it as an opportunity for growth and learning. By doing so, you are less likely to turn to addictive behaviors as a coping mechanism.

Similarly, instead of viewing social situations as overwhelming or anxiety-provoking, you can reframe them as opportunities for connection and growth. By changing your perception of these situations, you may be more likely to engage in healthy behaviors, rather than turning to addictive ones to cope.

Reframing is a powerful tool for ending addiction. By shifting your mindset from one of helplessness to empowerment and changing the way you perceive triggers and situations associated with addiction, you create new paths for action and give yourself the best chance at overcoming addictive behaviors once and for all.

Chunking to Help End Addiction

Another technique that has proven to be highly effective in tackling addiction is chunking. Overcoming addiction requires a multifaceted approach that addresses every area of life. Tackling all of these areas can seem overwhelming and even impossible. Instead, chunking tasks into the categories of social, physical, emotional, mental, and spiritual aspects of life can make change more manageable.

Chunking involves breaking down aspects of addiction into small achievable goals and developing detailed plans for tackling each goal appropriately while staying focused on long-term success. By doing so, individuals can make progress toward recovery one step at a time.

Chunking works by breaking down the addiction, creating detailed plans for each aspect, and then celebrating success as we make progress.

Breaking Down Addiction

The first step in chunking is to break down addiction into its various components. For instance, if someone is addicted to drugs or alcohol, he may have social issues, such as strained relationships with friends and family members. He may also have physical problems, such as poor health due to substance abuse. He can have emotional issues, such as anxiety or depression and mental challenges, such as negative self-talk and limiting beliefs. Lastly, he could struggle with spiritual disconnection from their values or purpose in life.

By breaking down addiction into these smaller parts, it becomes easier to identify specific areas that need attention and create plans for addressing them individually.

Developing Detailed Plans

Once the various components of addiction are identified, the next step is to develop detailed plans for tackling each area specifically. This could involve setting small achievable goals such as attending a support group meeting once a week or exercising for 30 minutes every day.

Creating detailed plans helps you stay focused on your goals while avoiding overwhelming yourself with too much change all at once. It also allows you to track your progress over time and recognize positive steps taken toward recovery.

Celebrating Successes

Finally, chunking makes it easier to recognize positive steps taken toward recovery and celebrate successes along the way. Each small achievement serves as motivation for continuing the journey toward overcoming addiction. This is why many support groups will celebrate sobriety milestones, such as 30, 60, and 90 days in recovery.

Chunking is a powerful technique that can help end addiction by breaking it down into smaller manageable pieces while creating detailed plans for tackling each area specifically. It will provide you with a roadmap toward recovery while allowing you to celebrate successes along the way.

Auditory Distraction to Help End Addiction

Another technique that has proven to be highly effective in tackling the social, physical, emotional, mental, and spiritual aspects of addiction is auditory distraction.

Auditory distraction involves using soothing noises such as classical music or ocean waves to distract your brain from intense cravings. This technique can help lower anxiety levels and reduce stress, making it easier for individuals to resist the urge to relapse.

Lowering Anxiety Levels

When someone experiences intense cravings for drugs or alcohol, their anxiety levels can skyrocket. The body goes into fight or flight mode, making it difficult to think clearly and make rational decisions. Using auditory distraction can help lower anxiety levels by providing a calming presence in the environment. Soothing sounds like classical music or ocean waves have been shown to have a calming effect on the mind and body, reducing feelings of stress and anxiety.

Distracting the Brain

Another way auditory distraction helps end addiction is by distracting the brain from intense cravings. When individuals listen to calming sounds, they shift their focus away from their cravings and toward something more peaceful. This shift in focus can make it easier for individuals to resist the urge to relapse because their attention is no longer solely focused on their addiction.

Improving Mood

Auditory distraction can improve mood by releasing dopamine in the brain. Dopamine is a neurotransmitter associated with pleasure and reward. By listening to calming sounds like classical music or ocean waves, individuals can trigger dopamine release in their brains without turning to drugs or alcohol. This release of dopamine improves mood and provides individuals with a sense of pleasure they may be seeking through substance abuse.

Auditory distraction is another valuable technique for ending addiction. It helps lower anxiety levels, distracts the brain from cravings, and improves mood without relying on drugs or alcohol.

Using Anchoring to Achieve a Recovery Mindset

Another technique that has proven to be highly effective in achieving a recovery mindset is creating anchors for specific states of being that help keep you focused on ending any addiction.

Anchoring involves using certain cues using your five senses such as auditory, kinesthetic, olfactory (smell), gustatory (taste), or visual images to help bring yourself back into alignment when faced with temptation or difficulty in managing cravings and negative thoughts related to the addiction process. This technique can help individuals quickly achieve emotional balance during particularly challenging times.

Anchoring works by remembering a specific time when you felt happy, confident, secure, motivated, or any other state that you may want to achieve when feeling at risk of falling back into your addiction. By remembering these states—seeing what you saw, hearing what you heard, and feeling what you felt—you can recreate that same feeling anytime you wish.

Creating Anchors

The first step in anchoring is creating the anchor(s). An anchor is simply a cue that triggers a specific emotional response. For instance, you may choose to associate the smell of lavender with feelings of calmness.

Other common anchors include visual images, such as pictures or objects, auditory cues such as music or sounds, and kinesthetic cues such as touch or movement.

To create an anchor, you should choose a specific cue that you want to associate with a particular emotional state.

Using Anchors

Once you have created an anchor, you can use it in challenging times associated with overcoming your addiction. For instance, if you are experiencing cravings for drugs or alcohol, you could use your anchor to bring yourself back into alignment to dismiss the craving.

To use an anchor, you will focus on the cue associated with the emotional state you want to achieve. You should allow yourself to fully experience the emotion associated with the anchor while also focusing on their breath and physical sensations in your body.

This technique can help you quickly achieve emotional balance during particularly challenging times, providing you with a tool for shifting your focus away from your addiction and toward more positive emotions.

Benefits of Anchoring

There are several benefits of using anchoring as part of a strategy for overcoming addiction. Firstly, it provides you with a quick way of achieving emotional balance when faced with temptation or difficulty in managing cravings and negative thoughts. Secondly, it helps to shift attention away from cravings and negative thoughts associated with addiction toward more positive emotions. Lastly, it can serve as a reminder of why you are working toward recovery in the first place.

Emotional Freedom Technique (EFT)-Energy Tapping

EFT is a form of "energy psychology" that releases blocked energy by tapping on acupressure points along the body while at the same time focusing on specific thoughts or emotions related to the desired outcome. The technique involves tapping on pressure points of the body while focusing on negative emotions and thoughts, allowing you to release suppressed emotions and disruptive patterns. This encourages an alignment between physical and emotional states while also decreasing stress levels associated with addiction.

EFT has been proven effective in helping individuals end their addiction and gain greater control over their day-to-day lives. It will help you recognize your addictive behavior and more effectively manage it so that you can break free from its hold over you. By using EFT, you can tap into your inner resources and find the strength to take back control of your life.

Tapping into the Power of EFT enhanced with principles of EMI

1. Identify the most significant issue to be addressed in this moment.
2. Take a 1 to 10 rating of the intensity of this issue at the moment.
3. Call out the issue while tapping the karate chop point on the hand.
4. Do THREE rounds of tapping through the eight tapping points:
   - Top/crown of the head
   - Inside Eyebrow
   - Side of Eye
   - Under Eye
   - Under nose
   - Between bottom lip and chin
   - Collarbone
   - Under arm

Round #1: Call out the issue: "Even though I am experiencing this discomfort, I fully and completely accept myself."

Take a 1-10 Rating of your ISSUE between each round of tapping.

Round #2: Release the issue: I am releasing this

discomfort now. All discomfort is leaving my body. My mind is focused on positive thoughts, I banish this discomfort now, etc.

Take a 1-10 Rating of your ISSUE between each round of tapping.

Round #3: Speak in the positive: I am getting happier by the moment. I have much to be happy about. I feel joy entering my spirit. I feel calm and relaxed, etc.

Lock in the change with an EMI/EFT Sequence. I have found the following sequence to be extremely helpful in locking in the changes achieved while tapping. The sequence incorporates principles from EFT, EMI, and other approaches as a powerful closing sequence to each energy tapping intervention. The sequence uses the gamut point, located on the back of either hand between the knuckles at the base of the ring finger and the little finger. Many EFT practitioners refer to this as the 9 Gamut Procedure.

While tapping the Gamut point continuously, perform the following actions:

1. Close your eyes.
2. Open your eyes.
3. With your head held steady, look hard down to the right.

4. With your head held steady, look hard down to the left.
5. With your head held steady, roll your eyes clockwise in a circle.
6. With your head held steady, roll your eyes counterclockwise in a circle.
7. Hum 3-4 seconds of a song (e.g., "Happy Birthday").
8. Count rapidly from 1 to 5.
9. Hum the same 3-4 seconds of the song again.

Overall, these techniques can be very useful tools in helping individuals overcome their addictions and reclaim their lives. With dedication, commitment, and practice, it is possible to use them to break free from any kind of addiction!

Chapter 11: Effective Therapeutic Approaches to End Any Addiction

There are several effective therapeutic approaches that can help individuals end their addiction for good. These interventions are best implemented with the assistance of a trained practitioner who has experience in helping people overcome addiction.

Some of the most effective therapeutic approaches to end any addiction are Conversational Hypnosis, Eye Movement Integration (EMI), Time Transformation Therapy, and Hypnotherapy.

Using Conversational Hypnosis to End Addiction

Conversational hypnosis is a powerful tool used in therapy to help individuals break free from their addictions, obsessions, and compulsions. This approach involves creating a relaxed state of mind in the individual through conversational language patterns and suggestions. By doing so, the practitioner can help the individual access their subconscious mind where they can identify and address the root cause of their addiction.

Through conversational hypnosis sessions, individuals better understand the structure of their addiction and what root cause issues need to be addressed to eliminate the addiction. They learn how to change negative thought patterns and behaviors associated with their addiction. This approach helps them develop new coping mechanisms which enable them to overcome cravings and triggers effectively.

How Does Conversational Hypnosis Work?

Conversational hypnosis works by using language patterns and suggestions that bypass an individual's conscious mind and reach their subconscious mind directly, thereby loosening an individual's attachment to the addiction. The subconscious mind is where deep-seated beliefs about oneself reside, including those related to addictive behavior.

During conversational hypnosis sessions, practitioners

use carefully crafted language patterns that create a relaxed state of mind in the individual. This relaxed state enables them to tap into their subconscious mind more easily; allowing them to identify root causes, limiting beliefs, and underlying issues related to their addiction.

Once these issues are identified, practitioners use further language patterns and suggestions aimed at changing negative thought patterns associated with addictive behavior. Over time these changes become fully integrated into an individual's subconscious mind leading them toward long-term recovery from their addiction.

Benefits of Using Conversational Hypnosis for Addiction Treatment

There are several benefits of using conversational hypnosis as part of an addiction recovery plan:

1. Customized Therapeutic Approach
   Conversational hypnosis allows practitioners to tailor each session according to an individual's unique needs and situation. Each session is designed specifically for the patient based on what they need at that moment in time.
2. Non-Invasive Approach

Unlike other forms of therapy, such as medication or surgery, conversational hypnosis is non-invasive and does not require any physical intervention.

3. Long-Lasting Results
   Because conversational hypnosis aims at changing deep-seated beliefs about oneself, its effects tend to be long-lasting even after treatment has ended.

Conversational hypnosis is a powerful tool used in Personal Transformation Therapy to help individuals break free from addictive behavior patterns. Personal transformation therapy is an integrative approach to healing that draws on a variety of modalities, including psychotherapy, mindfulness practices, energy work, and more. The goal of this type of therapy is to help individuals identify and release negative patterns and beliefs that are holding them back from living their best life. By using techniques like guided visualization and meditation, clients are able to tap into their inner wisdom and make positive changes in their lives.

Conversational hypnosis creates a relaxed state of mind in the individual through carefully crafted language patterns and suggestions aimed at changing negative thought patterns associated with addictive behavior. By tapping into an individual's subconscious mind directly, practitioners can help patients identify underlying issues related to their addiction while also developing new coping mechanisms which enable them to overcome cravings and triggers effectively.

During a recent clinical intake session, as the client sat across from me, I began to use my conversational hypnosis approach. My words were carefully chosen, and my tone was soothing as I guided him through the intake interview.

At first, he seemed skeptical and somewhat perplexed as the interview was very different from what he was used to when seeking psychotherapy in the past. But as I continued with the use of subtle language patterns, I could see a shift in his thinking. His eyes became clearer and more focused, and his body relaxed into the chair. As we talked further, he opened up about some deep-seated fears and anxieties that had been holding him back for years, discussing issues comfortably during our first session that he had not shared previously with any other therapist. With each passing moment, those fears seemed to fade away, and he intuitively knew they no longer had the power over him that they once held.

By the end of our session, the client was practically glowing with newfound confidence and positivity. He left my office feeling like a weight had been lifted from his shoulders and all because of the power of conversational hypnosis.

This client and many others have been able to make meaningful shifts in their own life through this powerful technique. With the careful and subtle use of language patterns, clients are quickly able to unlock new levels of thinking, feeling, and acting that they never thought possible. New neural pathways are literally being blazed that were previously not available leading to new ways of thinking and being.

Eye Movement Integration (EMI): A Promising Therapy for Addiction Recovery

Despite the wide range of treatments available for addiction, relapse rates remain high, highlighting the need for innovative and effective therapies. One such approach is Eye Movement Integration (EMI), a promising therapeutic technique gaining popularity in addiction recovery.

What is EMI?

Eye Movement Integration (EMI) is a form of therapy that uses eye movements to stimulate both sides of the brain while recalling unresourceful states related to addiction. Individuals access the mind in ways that allow them to find internal resources they had long ago abandoned while imprisoned in addiction. This technique helps integrate traumatic experiences and significant emotional events related to addiction, giving individuals better access to resources needed for recovery.

The main goal of EMI is to reset the nervous system by calming it down from three different areas: cognitive, emotional, and somatic. Eye movement helps in reducing symptoms such as anxiety, depression, Post Traumatic Stress Disorder (PTSD), and addiction. The combination of physical movement and the focus on a specific stimulus provides the person with a sense of calmness and allows them to move out of the mental loops or patterns that are preventing them from moving forward in life.

During an EMI session, a therapist guides an individual through eye movements while they recall unresourceful states related to their addiction. The eye movements help process these experiences; reducing negative feelings and enabling individuals to let go of past traumas.

How Does EMI Help in Addiction Recovery?

EMI offers several benefits that make it an effective approach to treating addiction:

1. Integrating Traumatic Experiences

Traumatic experiences often underlie addictive behaviors. By integrating these experiences during EMI therapy, individuals can gain better access to resources needed for recovery.

2. Reducing Negative Emotions

Negative emotions, such as shame, guilt, and fear, are common triggers for addictive behaviors. EMI helps to reduce these negative feelings by processing traumatic experiences associated with addiction.

3. Enhancing Resources

EMI allows individuals to tap into internal resources such as resilience, strength, and empowerment needed for successful recovery.

****

My client Karen had been struggling with anxiety and depression for nearly two decades. She had tried everything from therapy to medication, but nothing seemed to work. That is until she heard about Eye Movement Integration (EMI) from another of my clients.

Skeptical at first, Karen decided to give it a try. She booked a session with me and came in with an open mind. During the session, I guided Karen through a series of eye movements while she focused on her unresourceful emotions and memories. To her surprise, Karen felt a sense of relief almost immediately. After just one session, Karen felt like a weight had been lifted off her shoulders. Her anxiety and depression were now manageable, and they no longer controlled her life. She was able to enjoy simple things like going for walks and spending time with loved ones without feeling overwhelmed.

Karen continued to use EMI as part of her mental health routine while also working with me through Time Transformation Therapy, and mindfulness approaches. Karen's life transformation was not only remarkable but inspiring to many others.

****

The Effectiveness of EMI

Several studies have shown the effectiveness of EMI in treating addiction. In one study conducted on veterans with PTSD and substance abuse disorders, participants who received EMI showed significant reductions in PTSD symptoms compared to those who did not receive therapy. Another study showed that individuals with alcohol use disorder who received EMI, had significantly lower cravings and fewer days of alcohol use compared to those who did not receive therapy.

Eye Movement Integration (EMI) offers a promising solution for the complex issue of addiction by integrating traumatic experiences, reducing negative emotions associated with past trauma, and enhancing internal resources necessary for recovery.

Time Transformation Therapy: Ending Addictions for Good

Time Transformation Therapy (TTT) is a powerful and transformational form of therapy that can help individuals break free from their addictive patterns and create lasting change in their lives.

It is an innovative approach to therapy that combines psychotherapy, hypnotherapy, and energy psychology to access the subconscious mind and create deep-rooted changes in a person's beliefs, thoughts, emotions, and behaviors. This type of therapy is highly effective in addressing underlying issues that often contribute to the development of addiction, as well as physical and emotional problems.

One of the most significant benefits of TTT is its ability to bridge the gap between the conscious and subconscious mind. The subconscious mind controls our automatic thoughts, emotions, and behaviors. By accessing this part of our mind through hypnosis or other techniques used in TTT, we can uncover limiting beliefs and negative patterns that contribute to addiction.

Time Transformation Therapy has the ability to eliminate stored negative emotions at the root cause, which can greatly relieve individuals of the burden associated with these negative emotions. This is especially important for those struggling with addiction, as many addictive behaviors stem from a desire to escape from uncomfortable feelings and emotions. By addressing these negative emotions through TTT, individuals can reduce their need for escapism and find healthier ways to cope with stressors. By accessing the subconscious mind and reprogramming limiting beliefs and patterns, TTT helps individuals release negative emotions that have been stored within them for years. This results in a greater sense of inner peace, clarity, and emotional stability, reducing their reliance on addictive behaviors as a coping mechanism.

Through TTT sessions, individuals can reprogram their subconscious mind with positive affirmations and beliefs that support their recovery journey. These changes not only help individuals overcome addiction but also improve their overall mental health and wellbeing.

Another benefit of TTT is its empowering nature.

Addiction can leave individuals feeling powerless and out of control. TTT can help these individuals take control over their thoughts, emotions, and behaviors by teaching them how to manage stressors effectively. Time Transformation Therapy is a powerful tool for ending addictions once and for all. Its unique combination of psychotherapy, hypnotherapy, and energy psychology allows for deep-rooted changes to take place in a person's subconscious mind.

****

Maria was a successful businesswoman in her mid-thirties. She had been struggling with an addiction to alcohol for years, and had tried everything to quit, but the addiction always came back.

She learned about Time Transformation Therapy (TTT) and decided to give it a try. During the first session, I carefully listened to Maria's struggles with addiction and how it had affected different aspects of her life. We began with a deep relaxation exercise that allowed her to access her subconscious mind. Then, we used hypnotic techniques to uncover the root cause of her addiction, which turned out to be related to her childhood trauma.

Using energy psychology, we released the negative emotions that were attached to the trauma and neutralized them. Afterward, we used positive affirmations to instill new beliefs in her subconscious mind.

The transformation was visible right after the first session. Maria started feeling more motivated and in control, and her desire for alcohol decreased significantly. Over the following weeks, we continued to work together and each session brought her closer to the healing she needed. She was able to explore and address the underlying emotional triggers contributing to her addiction.

By the end of the sixth session, Maria felt confident she could overcome her addiction, and she was right. She has been sober for over a year now!

TTT helped Maria make deep-rooted changes in her subconscious mind that allowed her to overcome her addiction once and for all. It has been a life-changing experience for her, and she recommends TTT to anyone struggling with addiction.

****

Hypnotherapy: A Powerful Approach to Recovering from Addiction

Whether it's substance abuse, gambling, sex, gaming, depression, food, grief, or some other addiction, breaking free from these patterns can be incredibly difficult. Traditional therapies like talk therapy or medication have largely failed and have rarely produced the life change needed.

Hypnotherapy, on the other hand, is an alternative therapeutic approach that has shown transformational results in treating addiction. It utilizes hypnotic trance states to access deeper levels of consciousness where one can overcome unwanted patterns or habits.

So, how does hypnotherapy work? During a hypnosis session, a trained therapist guides the client into a relaxed state of mind and heightened suggestibility. In this state, the therapist can offer suggestions that help shift negative thought patterns, release stubborn emotional states, and shift behavioral patterns related to addiction.

Hypnotherapy can also be used in combination with other therapies such as Eye Movement Integration (EMI) and Time Transformation Therapy (TTT). Together with hypnotherapy, these techniques help deepen relaxation, shift perspectives around addiction, and create lasting positive changes in personal behavior – all of which are essential for overcoming an addiction successfully.

One of the significant benefits of hypnotherapy is its

ability to tap into the subconscious mind where many addictive behaviors are rooted. Through guided visualizations and positive affirmations in a hypnotic trance state, clients can reprogram their subconscious minds with new beliefs and thought patterns that support sobriety.

It's important to note that hypnotherapy is not a magic wand that will instantly cure any addiction. Like any therapeutic approach, it requires commitment and active participation from both the client and the therapist. However, when used as part of a comprehensive treatment plan tailored to an individual's needs, hypnotherapy has proven effective in helping people break free from addictions once thought impossible to overcome.

By following these steps and getting support from professionals, you will be able to end your addiction quickly and easily without going through unpleasant withdrawal symptoms or risking relapse. Remember, take things one step at a time and don't be afraid to ask for help when needed.

SECTION FOUR: UNDERSTANDING RELAPSE PREVENTION

Chapter 12: Setting an Intention for the Life You Want to Live After You Recover

Ending an addiction is a difficult and courageous journey. It takes a tremendous amount of effort, strength, and support to overcome every addiction and live in freedom. But once you reach sobriety, your life starts anew. You have a chance to create the life you want to live, free from the shackles of addiction. Setting an intention can help you achieve that.

Setting an intention means making a conscious decision about the direction you want your life to take. It's not just about setting goals or making plans; it's about focusing on what matters most to you and aligning your actions with those values.

Here are some steps you can take to set an intention for the life you want after ending your addiction:

1. Reflect on your values

2. Imagine your ideal life

3. Set specific goals for your life

4. Take action

Reflect on Your Values to Set an Intention for the Life You Want After Conquering Your Addiction

Setting an intention for the life you want after ending addiction is a powerful way to create a fulfilling and meaningful future. However, before you can set this intention, it's important to reflect on your values. This means taking time to think about what's important to you in life so that you can align your actions with those values.

Here are some steps you can take to reflect on your values:

- Make a list of what motivates and inspires you
  Think about the things in life that make you feel alive, motivated, and inspired. These could be personal goals, relationships, hobbies, or anything else that brings joy and fulfillment.
- Identify your core values
  Once you have a list of what motivates and

inspires you, think about the underlying values these things represent. For example, if spending time with family brings joy and fulfillment, then family may be one of your core values.

- Consider how your current lifestyle aligns with your core values
Reflect on how your current lifestyle aligns with your core values. Are there areas where you're living out of alignment with what matters most to you? If so, think about how you can make changes to bring more alignment into your life.

- Write down your intentions based on your core values
Finally, use what you've learned from reflecting on your values to set an intention for the life you want after ending addiction. Write down specific intentions aligned with your core values and will help bring more fulfillment and joy into your life.

Remember, reflection is an ongoing process that requires honesty and self-awareness. It's important not to judge yourself or feel guilty if there are areas where you're not currently living in alignment with your core values. Instead, use this reflection as an opportunity for growth and change.

Reflecting on your values is a crucial step in setting an

intention for the life you want after ending addiction. By making a list of what motivates and inspires you, identifying your core values, considering how they align with your current lifestyle, and writing down specific intentions based on those values, you will be able to create a fulfilling future for yourself.

Imagine Your Ideal Life After Ending Your Addiction

Ending an addiction opens up endless possibilities for your future. Once you've overcome addiction, it's important to take time to imagine your ideal life and set intentions for the path ahead.

- Visualize where you want to live
  The first step in imagining your ideal life after ending addiction is to visualize where you want to live. This could be in a specific city or country, near family or friends, or in a peaceful and natural environment. Picture the type of home or apartment you would like to live in, along with any other details that are important to you.
- Consider what kind of work you want to do
  What kind of work do you see yourself doing? Do you have a dream job or career that you've always wanted? Maybe there's a creative passion or hobby that could turn into a fulfilling career if given the chance. Think about what kind of work

would bring you joy and fulfillment every day.
- Reflect on who you want in your social circle
When imagining your ideal life after recovery, it's important to think about who you want in your social circle. Surrounding yourself with supportive people, who share similar values, can make all the difference in creating a fulfilling future.
- Envision how you will spend your leisure time
Finally, envision how you will spend your leisure time in your ideal life after conquering your addiction. Will you engage in hobbies or activities that bring joy and relaxation? Perhaps there are new skills or experiences that you have always wanted to try but never had the opportunity to have before.

Imagining your ideal life after ending your addiction is an essential step toward creating a fulfilling future for yourself. By taking time to visualize these aspects of your ideal life, you can gain clarity on what matters most to you and create actionable steps toward living this vision. You will then be able to set clear intentions for the path ahead.

Setting Specific Goals for a Life Free from Addiction

It's not enough to simply imagine your ideal life post-addiction; you also need to set specific goals that will help get you there. Now that you have identified your values and imagined your ideal life, here are some tips for setting goals that are measurable and achievable.

- Set measurable goals
  When setting goals, it's crucial they are measurable. This means that you should be able to track progress toward achieving them. For example, if one of your goals is to improve your physical health, a measurable goal might be running a 5k within six months.
- Set achievable goals
  While it's important to challenge yourself with ambitious goals, it's equally important they are achievable. Setting unrealistic goals can lead to frustration and discouragement, which could ultimately derail your progress. Be honest with yourself about what is feasible given where you are currently in the recovery process.
- Mix short-term and long-term goals
  It's important to have a mix of short-term and long-term goals. Short-term goals can provide quick wins and keep motivation high, while long-

term goals provide direction and purpose over the long haul. Make sure each goal supports the larger vision for the life you want to lead after ending addiction.

Setting specific goals when setting an intention for a life free from addiction is essential in making progress toward achieving a fulfilling lifestyle. Identifying values first before imagining an ideal life helps guide people to be the kind of person to which they aspire. As well, their future aspirations will serve as their foundation in creating measurable and achievable short-term and long-term objectives toward being sober and truly free from any addictions.

Take Action Toward a Life Free from Addiction

Setting an intention for the life you want to live after ending addiction is just the first step. The real work begins when you start taking action toward achieving those goals. Here are some tips for taking action and making progress toward the life you want to lead.

- Create a daily routine
  One of the most effective ways to take action toward your goals is by creating a daily routine that supports your intentions. This could include

things like exercise, meditation, journaling, or spending time with supportive friends and family members. By building these habits into your daily routine, you'll be more likely to stay on track and make progress.

- Seek out new opportunities
Another way to take action is by looking for new opportunities that align with your values and support your goals. This could mean volunteering for a cause you care about, taking classes or workshops to learn new skills, or joining a support group for people in recovery. These experiences can help broaden your perspective and provide new avenues for growth.

- Connect with others
Connecting with others who share similar values, can also be a powerful motivator in moving toward your goals. Whether it's through online communities, support groups, or social events, finding like-minded individuals can provide encouragement and accountability as you work toward building the life you want.

- Practice Self-compassion
Finally, it's important to practice self-compassion as you navigate the ups and downs of recovery and work toward your goals. Remember, setbacks

are normal and part of the process. Don't beat yourself up if things do not go according to plan. Instead, focus on what you have learned from those experiences and use them as fuel for continued growth.

In conclusion, setting intentions is only half the battle; taking consistent actions every day will help bring those intentions into fruition. Creating daily routines that align with personal values can help build momentum while seeking out new opportunities broadens perspectives which helps create new avenues for growth. Connecting with others who share similar values provides encouragement and accountability. Practicing self-compassion acknowledges setbacks as part of the process, and focusing on lessons learned from these experiences serves as fuel for continued growth.

Remember that setting an intention is not a one-time event; it's an ongoing process that requires commitment and dedication. By staying focused on what matters most to you and taking consistent action toward those goals, you can create the life you want after ending your addiction.

Setting an intention for the life you want after ending your addiction is a powerful tool for achieving lasting change. By taking the steps outlined, you can create a fulfilling and meaningful future for yourself. Be sure to take some time today to set an intention for the life of sobriety that awaits!

Chapter 13: Permanent Relapse Prevention Strategies After Ending an Addiction

Ending an addiction is a significant accomplishment that requires a lot of hard work, dedication, and support. However, staying sober is an ongoing process that requires continued effort and commitment. Without it, there is always a risk of relapse. Relapse can be devastating to someone who has worked hard to overcome addiction. However, there are strategies that can help you prevent relapse and maintain sobriety for the long haul.

Knowing Your Triggers

Knowing your triggers is an essential part of preventing

relapse in addiction recovery. By identifying them and developing strategies for managing them, you'll be better equipped to stay sober over the long term.

Triggers are people, places, or things that make you want to use drugs or alcohol again. They can be internal or external factors that cause cravings and lead to relapse. For example, a trigger could be a stressful situation at work, hanging out with old friends who still use drugs or alcohol, or even a specific smell that reminds you of using substances.

Knowing your triggers is essential because they can catch you off guard and cause you to slip back into old habits. By identifying your triggers and avoiding them as much as possible, you'll be better equipped to stay sober. It is important to remember that everyone's triggers are different, so what might be a trigger for one person may not be for another.

Identifying your triggers takes time and self-reflection. You can start by keeping a journal of when and where cravings occur. Note any feelings or thoughts that come up when you experience those cravings. Over time, patterns will emerge, which will help you identify your specific triggers.

You can also seek support from counselors or peer

groups who specialize in addiction recovery. They can help guide you through the process of identifying your triggers and provide strategies for managing them.

Once you have identified your triggers, it's important to have a plan for managing them. Here are some strategies that may help:

- Avoiding high-risk situations
  If there are certain people or places that trigger cravings for drug or alcohol use, try to avoid them as much as possible.
- Practicing self-care
  Taking care of yourself physically and mentally is crucial in managing triggers. This includes getting enough sleep, eating well-balanced meals, exercising regularly, and practicing relaxation techniques like meditation.
- Developing coping skills
  Coping skills such as deep breathing exercises or positive self-talk can help manage cravings when they arise.
- Seeking support
  Lean on supportive friends and family members who understand what you are going through. Joining a recovery group can also provide valuable support in managing triggers.

Practicing Mindfulness

Addiction relapse is a common struggle for those in recovery. It's easy to fall back into old habits and negative thought patterns, especially when faced with stress and triggers. However, practicing mindfulness can be a powerful tool for preventing relapse.

Mindfulness is the practice of being present in the moment without judgment. It involves focusing your attention on your thoughts, feelings, and physical sensations in the present moment. By doing so, you become more aware of your thoughts and emotions and can better manage them.

Here are some ways that mindfulness can help prevent addiction relapse:

- Reducing stress
  Stress is a major trigger for addiction relapse. When you're stressed, it's easy to turn to drugs or alcohol as a way to cope. However, practicing mindfulness can help reduce stress by allowing you to focus on the present moment instead of worrying about the future or dwelling on the past.
- Managing cravings
  Cravings are another common trigger for addiction relapse. When you experience a craving,

it's easy to give in and use drugs or alcohol again. By practicing mindfulness, you can learn how to observe your cravings without acting on them. This allows you to ride out the craving until it passes.

- Improving emotional regulation
Emotional dysregulation is common among those in recovery from addiction. Negative emotions like anger, sadness, and anxiety can easily lead to relapse if not managed properly. Mindfulness helps improve emotional regulation by allowing you to observe your emotions without judgment and respond to them in a healthy way.
- Increasing self-awareness
Self-awareness is key to preventing addiction relapse. By becoming more aware of your thoughts and emotions, you can better understand what triggers your addictive behaviors and how to avoid them. Mindfulness helps increase self-awareness by bringing your attention back to the present moment instead of getting lost in negative thoughts or memories.

Exercising

Regular exercise can be a powerful tool for preventing

relapse. Exercise is not only good for your physical health but also your mental health. Regular exercise can help reduce stress levels and boost mood, making it easier to stay sober. Here are some ways that exercise can help prevent addiction relapse:

- Reducing stress
  When you're stressed, it can be easy to return to addictive patterns as a way to cope. Regular exercise can help reduce stress by releasing endorphins, which are natural mood boosters.
- Boosting mood
  Mood disorders, such as depression and anxiety, are common among those in recovery from addiction. Regular exercise has been shown to improve symptoms of these disorders by boosting mood and reducing negative thoughts.
- Providing structure
  Structure is important for those in recovery from addiction. Regular exercise provides structure by creating a routine and giving you something positive to focus on each day.
- Improving self-esteem
  Low self-esteem is another common issue among those in recovery from addiction. Regular exercise can improve self-esteem by helping you feel better about yourself, both physically and

mentally.
- Creating social connections
  Social connections are important for maintaining sobriety. Regular exercise can create social connections by allowing you to join fitness classes or workout groups where you can meet like-minded individuals who share similar goals.

Regular exercise is an effective strategy for preventing addiction relapse. By reducing stress levels, boosting mood, providing structure, improving self-esteem, and creating social connections, regular exercise helps keep you focused on your goals and avoid negative thought patterns that could lead to relapse.

Getting Enough Sleep

Another aspect that is often overlooked, but plays a critical role in relapse prevention, is getting enough sleep. Adequate sleep is essential for overall health and wellbeing, and it can significantly impact an individual's ability to stay sober.

Lack of sleep can lead to increased stress levels, fatigue, and irritability, which are all factors that can contribute to relapse. When an individual is sleep-deprived, their cognitive abilities are impaired, making it difficult to make sound decisions or handle stressful situations effectively. Additionally, lack of sleep can weaken the immune system, leaving individuals more susceptible to illness or injury.

How sleep can help prevent relapse:
- Getting enough sleep is crucial for maintaining sobriety because it helps individuals better cope with stress and regulate their emotions.
- Well-rested individuals have better impulse control and decision-making abilities.
- Well-rested individuals are also more likely to engage in healthy activities, such as exercise and self-care.
- Getting enough sleep can also improve mental health by reducing symptoms of anxiety and depression. These conditions are common among those recovering from addiction and can increase the risk of relapse if left untreated.

Tips for better sleep
Getting restful sleep should be a top priority for those in recovery. Here are some tips to help you get the best sleep possible:

- Stick to a consistent sleep schedule.
- Create a relaxing bedtime routine.

- Avoid caffeine and nicotine before bed.
- Limit exposure to screens before bedtime.
- Make sure your sleeping environment is comfortable and conducive to restful sleep.

Prioritizing adequate rest through these strategies or others that work best for you will go a long way in preventing relapse. Getting enough quality sleep may seem like a simple thing but its importance cannot be overstated when it comes to addiction recovery. It has numerous benefits on both physical health as well as emotional wellbeing which play an important part in maintaining sobriety over the long term.

Eating a Clean and Healthy Diet while Avoiding Sugar

One aspect that is often overlooked, but plays a critical role in relapse prevention, is eating a clean and healthy diet. Recovery from addiction is a challenging process, and maintaining sobriety requires making a variety of lifestyle changes. Having a nutritious diet is one of the changes that can help improve overall health, reduce cravings for drugs or alcohol, and promote emotional well-being.

Research has shown that there is a strong connection between diet and addiction recovery. A clean, balanced diet can help reduce inflammation in the body, which can be beneficial for those who have damaged their physical health through substance abuse. Specific nutrients such as omega-3 fatty acids and amino acids like tryptophan are essential for brain function, which can aid in reducing cravings.

On the other hand, consuming unhealthy foods high in sugar or processed ingredients can cause fluctuations in blood sugar levels that may trigger cravings for drugs or alcohol. Sugar also activates similar brain pathways as addictive substances, leading to an increased risk of relapse.

Eating a clean and healthy diet can provide numerous benefits for those recovering from addiction. Here are some ways it can help prevent relapse:

- Reducing inflammation
  By consuming foods rich in antioxidants such as fruits, vegetables, nuts, and seeds you reduce inflammation caused by drug/alcohol abuse.
- Supporting brain function
  Nutrient-rich foods like salmon (omega-3) or turkey (tryptophan) support brain function which helps regulate mood swings.
- Reducing cravings
  Foods high in fiber, such as whole grains or beans, make you feel full longer and reduce cravings.

- Avoiding sugar
  Avoiding sugary foods and drinks reduces fluctuations of blood sugar levels, which helps keep your mind stable without triggering cravings.

Here are some tips to help you eat clean and healthily:

- Plan your meals ahead of time.
- Choose whole foods over processed ones.
- Eat more fruits and vegetables.
- Incorporate lean protein sources into your meals.
- Drink plenty of water throughout the day.

Eating a clean and healthy diet while avoiding sugar is an essential strategy for relapse prevention during addiction recovery. It provides numerous benefits beyond just physical health; it promotes emotional well-being by ensuring that your brain gets the necessary nutrients to support mood regulation while keeping cravings at bay.

Using Grounding Exercises

One strategy that can be particularly effective in preventing relapse is the use of grounding exercises. These techniques are designed to bring someone back into the present moment when they're feeling overwhelmed or triggered by something from their past or by thoughts of the future. Grounding exercises can help prevent relapse by helping to reduce anxiety levels.

Grounding exercises are simple techniques that can help you stay present and focused on the current moment. They're often used in therapy sessions to help people deal with anxiety, stress, or trauma. Some common grounding exercises include deep breathing, meditation, visualization, and physical activities, such as yoga or walking.

When you start to dwell on your past mistakes or feel overwhelmed by worries about the future, grounding exercises can help you stay focused on the present moment, reducing the likelihood of engaging in addictive behaviors.

By reducing anxiety levels, grounding exercises can also reduce cravings for drugs or alcohol. When you're feeling stressed or anxious, it's easy to turn to substances as a way to cope with those feelings. But, if you have tools like grounding techniques at your disposal, you'll be better equipped to manage those emotions without turning back to addictive behaviors.

If you're new to grounding exercises, here are some tips for getting started:

- Find a quiet space where you can focus without

distractions.
- Choose an exercise that feels comfortable for you. Whether it's deep breathing, meditation, visualization, or a physical activity like yoga or walking.
- Practice your chosen exercise regularly, ideally every day.
- Use your grounding exercise whenever you feel triggered or overwhelmed by thoughts of using drugs or alcohol again.

Remember that relapse prevention requires ongoing effort and commitment, but by incorporating grounding exercises into your daily routine, you'll be giving yourself an important tool for staying sober and focused on your recovery journey. Grounding exercises are powerful tools for addiction recovery and relapse prevention. By helping you stay present and focused on the current moment while reducing anxiety levels and cravings for addictive substances, these techniques can make all the difference in maintaining long-term sobriety.

Changing People/Places/Things

Sometimes changing people, places, or things in your life may be necessary to maintain sobriety long-term. If certain people or situations trigger cravings or negative emotions, it may be necessary to distance yourself from them.

Addiction is often linked to specific people, places, and things that trigger cravings for drugs or alcohol. These triggers can include social events where drugs or alcohol are present, certain relationships that encourage substance abuse behaviors, or even particular locations like bars and clubs.

If you're serious about maintaining sobriety long-term, it's important to identify these triggers and make changes accordingly. This could mean avoiding certain social events altogether or distancing yourself from relationships that encourage substance abuse behaviors. While making these changes might feel uncomfortable at first, they'll ultimately help you stay focused on your recovery journey.

Identifying people, places, and things that are triggers can be challenging, but it's an essential step toward maintaining sobriety long-term. Here are some questions you can ask yourself:

- Are there particular people in my life who encourage me to engage in addictive behaviors?
- Are there certain locations where I'm more likely

to use substances?
- Are there objects associated with my addiction that I need to get rid of?

By taking inventory of these potential triggers, you'll have a better understanding of what changes need to be made in your life.

Once you've identified the triggering people, places, and things in your life, it's time to make some changes. This might mean distancing yourself from toxic relationships entirely. This can sometimes be difficult if those individuals are family members or close friends. However, if someone's behavior is putting your sobriety at risk, then creating boundaries may be necessary for your continued recovery journey. Similarly, if there are specific locations where you're more likely to use substances—like bars and clubs—then avoiding those environments entirely could be crucial for your success in remaining sober. Lastly, getting rid of any objects associated with previous drug use can also help prevent relapse by removing visual reminders of past addictive behaviors.

While changing people, places, and things in our lives may seem daunting at first, it's often necessary for successful addiction recovery. By identifying triggering factors in our lives and making appropriate changes, we create an environment conducive to our continued success on the path toward lasting sobriety.

The Power of Gratitude in Addiction Recovery

Addiction recovery is a journey that can be challenging and overwhelming, making it easy to get caught up in negative thoughts and emotions associated with addiction. This mindset can make it difficult to stay motivated and committed to the recovery process. One way to shift your focus away from negativity and build resilience in recovery is by expressing gratitude daily.

Gratitude is the practice of acknowledging and appreciating the positive aspects of life. When you express gratitude, you shift your attention away from what's wrong or missing in your life, toward what's good and right. This helps create a more positive mindset, which can help you cope with the challenges of addiction recovery.

Here are some ways that expressing gratitude daily can benefit your addiction recovery:

- Helps you stay focused on your goals
  When you're going through addiction recovery, it's important to have clear goals and objectives. Expressing gratitude daily can help you stay

focused on those goals by reminding you of why you're working so hard to overcome addiction. By focusing on the positive aspects of life, such as supportive friends and family, good health, or new opportunities, you'll be more motivated to continue making progress toward your goals.

- Increases resilience
Recovery from addiction can be a bumpy road with many ups and downs along the way. By practicing gratitude regularly, you'll develop a greater sense of resilience that will help you bounce back from setbacks more easily. Gratitude helps cultivate a positive outlook on life which helps us look for solutions when faced with difficulties, instead of getting bogged down by them.

- Improves mental health
Addiction often occurs alongside mental health issues, such as anxiety or depression. Practicing gratitude has been shown to improve overall mental health by reducing stress levels and increasing feelings of positivity and contentment.

- Builds stronger relationships
Expressing gratitude isn't just beneficial for yourself; it can also strengthen relationships with others around you including family members,

friends or co-workers who support your recovery journey.

Developing a habit of expressing gratitude daily is an effective way to shift focus away from the negativity associated with addiction toward positive aspects of life. This helps build resilience in recovery over time. Regularly practicing gratitude creates an optimistic outlook that makes it easier to handle challenges while staying motivated toward achieving long-term goals in sobriety.

Developing Spirituality: A Key to Addiction Recovery

Addiction not only harms your physical and mental health but it also affects your relationships, livelihood, emotional development, and self-actualization. Addiction recovery requires a comprehensive approach that includes physical, emotional, and spiritual healing.

Developing spirituality does not necessarily mean becoming religious. Instead, it means finding meaning beyond yourself, which helps you find balance in life during addiction recovery. This helps you to find your purpose and access the highest version of yourself.

Spirituality and religion are often used interchangeably, but they are different concepts. Religion is an organized belief system with specific rituals, practices, and beliefs. Spirituality, on the other hand, is a personal experience that involves connecting with something greater than yourself.

While religion can be a source of spiritual connection for some individuals during addiction recovery, it may not be helpful for you if you have had negative experiences with organized religion or simply do not resonate with its teachings.

Developing spirituality during addiction recovery means finding meaning beyond yourself. This could involve connecting with nature, practicing mindfulness or meditation, volunteering in the community, or pursuing creative endeavors.

By finding meaning beyond yourself, you can shift the focus from your own struggles to something larger than yourself. This can help you gain perspective on your situation and find hope for the future.

Developing spirituality can also help you reach the highest version of yourself. By connecting with something greater than yourself, you can tap into your inner strength and resilience to continuously move toward self-actualization.

This allows you to face challenges head-on and make

positive changes in your life. You become more aware of your thoughts and emotions and learn to manage them in healthy ways. You begin to see yourself as part of a larger whole which gives you a sense of belonging and purpose.

Keeping Busy with Positive Activities in Addiction Recovery

One of the biggest challenges faced by those in recovery is filling the time once spent on addictive behaviors. This can be a daunting task, but it's essential to prevent relapse and advance in areas neglected during active addiction.

Keeping busy with positive activities, such as hobbies, family, career, school, or volunteer work helps provide purposeful engagement while also filling the void left by addictive behaviors. Here are some reasons why keeping busy with positive activities is crucial for successful recovery:

- Preventing relapse
  One of the main benefits of staying busy is that it helps prevent relapse. When you have idle time on your hands, it's easy to fall back into old habits and patterns. By keeping yourself engaged in

positive activities, you're less likely to have cravings or thoughts about using drugs or alcohol.

- Filling the void
  Addiction often takes over every aspect of your life, leaving little room for anything else. Once you enter recovery, there's often a void that needs to be filled. Engaging in positive activities provides a healthy outlet for your energy and helps fill that void.
- Advancing in neglected areas
  During active addiction, many areas of life are neglected. Relationships suffer, careers stall, and personal growth halts. Engaging in positive activities allows you to make progress in these areas while also building new skills and interests.
- Finding purpose
  Lastly, engaging in positive activities helps you find purpose outside of addiction. It gives you something to look forward to and work toward while providing meaning and fulfillment beyond addiction.

Keeping busy with positive activities is not only beneficial for those in recovery but also essential for successful long-term sobriety. Whether it's picking up a new hobby or volunteering at a local organization, finding ways to stay engaged will help fill the time once spent on addictive behaviors while providing purposeful engagement toward personal growth and advancement.

Strong Social Support Network

While individual willpower and determination are crucial during addiction recovery, having a strong social support network is equally vital for maintaining sobriety and avoiding relapse.

Here are some reasons why having a strong social support network is essential for successful recovery:

- Understanding and empathy
  Addiction can be isolating, leaving individuals feeling alone and misunderstood. Having a supportive community allows you to connect with others who understand what you're going through. They can offer empathy, encouragement, and non-judgmental support.
- Accountability
  A strong social support network provides accountability by holding you responsible for your actions. They can help keep you on track with your recovery goals while providing motivation to stay committed.
- Positive Influence

Surrounding yourself with people who are supportive of your recovery journey helps provide a positive influence on your life. It's easier to maintain sobriety when those around you are also committed to living a healthy lifestyle.

- Encouragement
  Recovery is not always easy and there may be times when you feel discouraged or overwhelmed. A supportive community can offer words of encouragement and remind you of how far you've come in your journey.
- Opportunities for Growth
  Having supportive friends and family members also provides opportunities for personal growth. You can learn new skills, try new hobbies, or take on new challenges that help build confidence and self-esteem.

Having a strong social support network is essential for maintaining sobriety and avoiding relapse. Surrounding yourself with people who understand what you're going through and who will support you in your recovery journey can make all the difference in achieving long-term success. Whether it's attending support groups or connecting with loved ones, building relationships that foster positivity and encouragement will help ensure sustained recovery.

There are various examples of social support networks for addiction recovery, each tailored to meet the unique needs and preferences of individuals in recovery. The best-known and most successful programs are 12-step programs, such as Alcoholics Anonymous (AA) and Narcotics Anonymous (NA). These programs provide a supportive community of peers who understand what it's like to struggle with addiction. These programs offer regular meetings where individuals can share their experiences, receive guidance, and find support from others who have faced similar challenges. Other forms of social support networks include sober living homes, online recovery communities, Celebrate Recovery, Rational Recovery, and SMART (Self-Management and Recovery Training) Recovery. Others find this same level of social support through family, church involvement, or community volunteerism. Whatever form of social support one chooses, building a strong network is essential for sustaining long-term sobriety.

Ending an addiction is just the beginning of long-term recovery; staying sober requires ongoing effort, commitment, and support. By implementing permanent relapse prevention strategies, such as knowing your triggers, practicing mindfulness, creating social support networks, and exercising, one increases their chances of remaining sober long term while improving quality of life overall!

Celebrating Success & Moving Forward

One of the most important steps in overcoming addiction is celebrating success. This means acknowledging and celebrating even small achievements along the way. It's important to remember that recovery is a journey, not a destination. Every step taken toward ending an addiction should be celebrated as a victory.

Celebrating success can help motivate you to continue on your path toward recovery. It can also help boost self-confidence and provide a sense of accomplishment. Recognizing progress made along the way can make the journey toward permanent recovery seem less daunting.

But celebrating success isn't enough on its own. To permanently end addiction, it's important to take proactive steps forward. This means creating a plan for continued sobriety and sticking to it. Using the strategies previously mentioned will help.

Remember - every step toward sobriety counts as a victory worth celebrating!

Chapter 14: The Pros and Cons of 12-Step Programs

12-step programs have been a cornerstone of addiction recovery for over 80 years. These programs, such as Alcoholics Anonymous (AA) and Narcotics Anonymous (NA), have helped countless individuals achieve sobriety and maintain long-term recovery.

The Oxford Group played a significant role in the formation of Alcoholics Anonymous. The group was a Christian organization that focused on spiritual practices and personal transformation. Bill Wilson, one of the co-founders of AA, was introduced to the Oxford Group during his stay at a hospital for alcoholism treatment. He became convinced that this spiritual approach was critical to his recovery and began sharing his experiences with others who were struggling.

The principles and practices of the Oxford Group heavily influenced the development of the 12-step program used by Alcoholics Anonymous. In particular, the idea of surrendering oneself to a higher power and working with others who have experienced similar struggles became central tenets of both organizations.

While AA eventually split from the Oxford Group due to disagreements over certain beliefs and practices, the latter's influence on the former cannot be overstated. Today, AA remains an organization that is heavily influenced by spiritual principles and continues to help millions find hope and healing in their journey toward sobriety.

Alcoholics Anonymous is a fellowship of individuals who come together to support one another in their journey toward sobriety. It was founded in 1935 by Bill Wilson and Dr. Bob Smith, two men who struggled with alcoholism themselves. They recognized the need for an organization that would provide support and guidance for those struggling with addiction.

The 12-Step program was developed by Alcoholics Anonymous to help people overcome addiction. It has since been adopted by other organizations as a way to address various forms of addiction, including drug abuse, gambling, and overeating.

The 12-Step program is based on spiritual principles and

encourages individuals to take responsibility for their lives and actions. Here's a breakdown of the 12 steps and how they work:

- Step 1: Admitting powerlessness over the addiction
  This can be difficult for some people because it requires acknowledging that they are not in control.
- Step 2: Believing in a higher power that can help with recovery
  The higher power does not have to be religious or even defined, but rather something greater than yourself.
- Step 3: Turning your life over to the higher power
  This means letting go of control and trusting that the higher power will guide you toward recovery.
- Step 4: Conducting a moral inventory
  In this step, you will conduct an honest self-assessment of your past behaviors and actions related to your addiction.
- Step 5: Admitting wrongs to yourself, others, and the higher power
  This can be difficult but it is necessary for healing and moving forward.
- Step 6: Being ready for change

In this step, you become ready for change and are willing to let go of old patterns of behavior.
- Step 7: Asking for help from the higher power
You will ask the higher power for help in removing character defects that contribute to addictive behavior.
- Step 8: Making amends
Make amends with those you have harmed through your addiction.
- Step 9: Making direct amends when possible without causing further harm.
- Step 10: Continuing self-assessment
In this step, you will continue with constant self-assessment and promptly admit when you are wrong or have made mistakes.
- Step 11: Seeking conscious contact with the higher power
You will do this through prayer or meditation.
- Step 12: Helping others in recovery
Once you have gone through recovery, you are encouraged to help others who are struggling with addiction.

Overall, the purpose of the twelve steps is not only about overcoming the addiction but also about personal growth and spiritual development. By following these steps, you can learn how to live a fulfilling life free from addiction.

However, like any tool in addiction recovery, the steps can be helpful or harmful depending on how they are used.

One potential pitfall of 12-step programs is the risk of feeding a person's addiction if not used carefully. While these programs provide a supportive community, structure, and guidance for recovery, some individuals may become too reliant on them as their sole source of support. They may attend meetings obsessively and fail to take action outside of meetings to work toward a self-actualized life.

****

Scott was a recent client who had struggled with alcohol addiction years ago and finally decided to attend Alcoholics Anonymous. There he found success in getting sober. However, as time went on, he realized that not much else had changed in his life. His marriage fell apart and he engaged in other problem behaviors such as overeating and gambling. He also struggled to advance in his career and just felt stuck in yet another cycle of feeling held back and unsuccessful.

Scott continued attending AA meetings, seven days a

week, for eight years. Despite the fact that Scott felt stuck and stagnant in his recovery journey, his AA support system continued to reinforce that AA attendance was the only way. Scott was told that only AA people would understand him, and he was even fed a stream of well-meaning slogans that continued to keep him stuck. Scott was told to "easy does it," "keep it simple (stupid)," "one day at a time," and "the program works for those who work it." Frustrated with this lack of progress, Scott eventually sought out help outside of AA through Personal Transformation Therapy. Through this therapy, Scott learned how to create the life he imagined recovery would bring.

He resolved old traumas that had been holding him back since childhood. He grew to understand the workings of his mind and how to step into the power of his subconscious mind. He learned to set an intention for the life he wanted and to focus on what he wanted in recovery rather than what he no longer wanted from his addiction. With this newfound knowledge, he was able to end every addiction that he had accumulated while in alcoholism recovery.

****

Scott's experience shows that while getting sober is an important first step, it's not always enough to fully transform one's life. Alcoholics Anonymous, while incredibly useful, can also become a people addiction that keeps people stuck. Often, additional work is needed to address underlying issues, resolve trauma, and create lasting change. With the right tools and support, anyone can overcome their struggles and achieve true transformation.

For decades, 12-step programs have been a go-to solution for people struggling with addiction. With millions of members worldwide, these programs provide a supportive community and a structured approach to recovery. However, as Scott discovered, there are some harmful slogans within these programs that can keep people stuck in their addiction.

"Easy does it" is a common phrase used in 12-step meetings to encourage members to take things slowly and not rush their recovery. While this may sound like good advice, it can also be used as an excuse for complacency. Some people interpret this slogan as meaning that they don't need to put in much effort to recover or that they should wait for things to get better on their own.

Another popular slogan is "Keep it simple (stupid)." This phrase is meant to remind members not to overthink their recovery and to focus on the basics. However, it can also be misinterpreted as meaning that members should only rely on the program's simple solutions and not seek more comprehensive treatment options.

"One day at a time" is perhaps the most well-known slogan of 12-step programs. It encourages members to focus on staying sober just for today, rather than worrying about the future or dwelling on the past. While this can be helpful for some people, others may use it as an excuse not to plan ahead or take action toward long-term goals.

"The program works for those who work it" is a slogan that suggests that the only way to succeed in recovery is by fully committing to the 12-step program's principles and practices. While dedication and hard work are important factors in any type of recovery, this phrase can also create feelings of shame and guilt among those who struggle with relapse or find certain aspects of the program challenging.

These slogans can contribute to a narrow-minded view of addiction treatment by suggesting that 12-step meetings are the only solution and that individualized care plans are unnecessary. They can also discourage critical thinking by promoting blind adherence to program principles without considering alternative approaches. Additionally, these slogans may make individuals feel like they're failing if they struggle with sobriety outside of meetings or if they choose other forms of treatment instead of relying solely on 12-step programs.

Slogans from 12-step programs can sometimes do more harm than good. To break free from harmful slogans and embrace a more integrated approach, individuals should consider seeking out professional help from therapists or addiction specialists who can offer more innovative and advanced approaches developed since AA started.

It's also important to remember that 12-step programs were designed to be completed in 90 days. This means that individuals were expected to complete all 12 steps within this timeframe. However, many people like Scott get stuck in a stagnating recovery program that fails to help them continue to grow, change, and move forward toward a fulfilling life.

While 12-step programs have been successful for many individuals battling addiction, there's no one-size-fits-all solution for everyone. Recovery is complex and multifaceted, requiring personalized care plans tailored to each individual's needs.

By embracing alternative approaches and seeking out personalized care plans based on scientific research rather than anecdotal evidence alone, we can create a more comprehensive system of support for those struggling with substance abuse disorders.

12-step programs like Alcoholics Anonymous have remained largely unchanged for almost a century. Advancements in our understanding of addiction, mental health, and neuroscience suggest that alternative or complementary approaches may be necessary to address the complexity of addiction.

Some newer approaches to addiction treatment focus on addressing underlying trauma or co-occurring mental health disorders that contribute to substance use disorders. These approaches recognize the interconnectedness of physical, emotional, and social health and aim to provide comprehensive care plans tailored to an individual's unique needs.

Mindfulness-based interventions, such as mindfulness-based stress reduction and mindfulness-based cognitive therapy, have become increasingly popular because of the transformational outcomes they produce in addiction treatment. These techniques promote self-awareness, emotional regulation, and stress reduction through meditation, breathing exercises, and other mindfulness practices.

Holistic approaches to addiction treatment recognize the interconnectedness of physical, emotional, social, and spiritual health. These approaches incorporate alternative therapies such as yoga, acupuncture, massage therapy, hypnotherapy, meditation, art therapy, or equine-assisted therapy into traditional treatment programs.

These innovative approaches offer personalized care plans tailored to an individual's unique needs rather than relying on a one-size-fits-all solution like 12-step programs. When these new models of care are paired with existing programs like 12-step meetings, those struggling with addictions are much more likely to gain a more comprehensive system of support.

Despite the criticisms of 12-step programs, it's worth noting that they remain a valuable resource for millions of people worldwide and can still be a component of a comprehensive approach, especially in the earliest days of addiction recovery. The supportive community and structured approach provided by these programs can be highly beneficial for those struggling with addiction as an adjunct to more innovative brain-based approaches like those outlined in this book.

The opportunity 12-step programs provide for individuals to connect with others who have shared experiences and struggles is invaluable. This sense of community can be incredibly powerful in maintaining sobriety.

Additionally, the structure provided by the program can help individuals establish healthy routines and habits. The step-by-step approach allows individuals to break down their recovery journey into manageable pieces.

Interesting note: While AA was originally developed specifically for individuals struggling with alcoholism, there are now variations of the program designed for other forms of addiction as well, such as Narcotics Anonymous (NA), Gamblers Anonymous (GA), Sex and Love Addicts Anonymous (SLAA), Overeaters Anonymous (OA), and many other programs.

Chapter 15: Wrapping it Up

Addiction can take hold of us in various forms, from substances to behaviors to thought patterns. However, addiction is not solely related to the substance or behavior itself but more about the underlying psychological and emotional factors that compel us to engage in such behaviors. In essence, we become addicted to ourselves, the self we have been programmed to be from a very early age as we learned coping mechanisms to deal with life's stresses.

The programming that leads to addiction can start as early as our time in the womb, with generational traumas, such as abuse, poverty, or addiction itself. These can be passed down from generation to generation shaping our earliest world experiences. Such traumas can influence our coping mechanisms for dealing with stress and emotions, making us more vulnerable to addictive behavior later in life. Thus, it is imperative to recognize the part that early experiences play in shaping our relationship with substances and behaviors to be able to overcome addiction patterns.

Some of us may engage in addictive behavior as a coping mechanism to relieve uncomfortable feelings, such as anxiety or depression. When we partake in behaviors that bring us joy or relieve stress, our brains secrete natural chemicals like dopamine that make us feel good. However, with time, repeated engagement in such behaviors may lead to a change in our brain structure, making us more sensitive to these pleasure-causing chemicals.

This sensitivity subsequently leads to a vicious cycle of addiction as we crave more intense experiences to achieve the same levels of pleasure-release from their pleasure centers. It can be challenging to get out of this cycle because our brains are wired to seek out pleasure and avoid pain.

Breaking free from addiction requires a significant shift in how we view ourselves and our relationship with the world. We need to restructure our brains in a way that leads to new outcomes and a new improved self-identity. Since addiction is fundamentally an addiction to oneself, we must carve out new neural pathways that help us achieve a healthier way of being. We do this by cultivating supportive relationships with like-minded individuals and adopting healthy coping mechanisms for dealing with stress and negative emotions. In addition, when we find meaning and purpose in life beyond addictive behaviors, we can reprogram ourselves toward a new and improved self.

To break free from addiction, it is crucial to rid your mind, body, and identity of every kind of addiction. We must not merely trade one addiction for another, but obliterate addiction from our system. This, in return, will eliminate anything that stands in the way of us becoming our new optimal selves. When we shed harmful and destructive behaviors and the old self that no longer serves us, we create a new identity. This new identity supports a healthy self-concept aligned with good health, success, prosperity, and freedom, enabling us to live life intentionally and purposefully.

www.ingramcontent.com/pod-product-compliance
Lightning Source LLC
Chambersburg PA
CBHW060319050426
42449CB00011B/2553